Investing
For the
Clueless

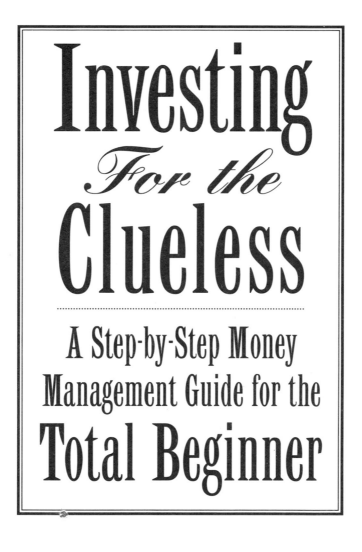

Investing
For the
Clueless

A Step-by-Step Money
Management Guide for the
Total Beginner

ALFRED M. WADDELL

A CITADEL PRESS BOOK
Published by Carol Publishing Group

Carol Publishing Group Edition, 1997

Originally published as *Sane Investing for the Non-Financial*

A Citadel Press Book
Published by Carol Publishing Group
Citadel Press is a registered trademark of Carol Communications, Inc.

Editorial, sales and distribution, rights and permissions inquiries
should be addressed to Carol Publishing Group, 120 Enterprise Avenue,
Secaucus, N.J. 07094

In Canada: Canadian Manda Group, One Atlantic Avenue, Suite 105,
Toronto, Ontario M6K 3E7

Carol Publishing Group books may be purchased in bulk at special
discounts for sales promotions, fund-raising, or educational purposes.
Special editions can be created to specifications. For details, contact :
Special Sales Department, Carol Publishing Group, 120 Enterprise Avenue,
Secaucus, N.J. 07094

Manufactured in the United States of America
10 9 8 7 6 5 4 3 2

Library of Congress Cataloging-in-Publication Data

Waddell, Alfred M. (Alfred Moore), 1939-
    Investing for the clueless : a step-by-step money management guide
  for the total beginner / Alfred M. Waddell.
        p.   cm.
    "A Citadel Press book."
    ISBN 0-8065-1768-9 (pbk.)
    1. Investments—United States. 2. Securities—United States.
HG4910.W238   1996
332.6—dc20   95-47089
                                                   CIP

ACKNOWLEDGMENTS

This was written at the encouragement of my wife, Clara, who suffered through my working nights and weekends as she acted as coach, word processor and critic. It would not have been possible without the experience gained working with Bill Wunderlich, Phyllis Scruggs, and our valued clients to solve their myriad financial problems.

The cartoons which bring good humor to a serious subject were contributed by Sam Ray who understands the very human problems that investors encounter.

Last but not least, I must thank Emily Yellin who edited and organized the material with great skill.

DISCLAIMER

Great care has been exercised in making this book factually accurate. The suggestions, opinions, and conclusions of the author are his own and subject to revision. For simplicity, examples, tables, and rates of return are all presented before the effects of state and federal income taxes.

The reader is urged to consult competent legal and financial counsel in developing investment strategies and not to rely on this text as a substitute for professional advice.

TABLE OF CONTENTS

INTRODUCTION

Introduction

Through many years as a professional investment advisor I've encountered highly intelligent people who are what I call "non-financial." In other words, they have money to invest, but they don't have a clue when it comes to making money investing. They are unprepared by either education, experience, or temperament to deal with the complex world of money management. As an insider in that world, I am writing this book to teach the non-financial its essentials.

I am neither a student, a professor, nor a journalist. I am a practicing investment advisor and the head of a registered investment advisory firm, Waddell and Associates, Inc. I started the firm in 1985 after retiring in my early forties from years of managing public companies. In my earlier career, I dealt with Wall Street as a corporate investment banking client, and oversaw the successful investment of tens of millions of dollars of pension funds. I gained a wealth of experience which I use daily at Waddell and Associates where we currently oversee approximately one hundred million dollars worth of investments for a variety of clients from all walks of life and with many different investment objectives.

A portion of our clients are individual investors with little or no investment experience. Some are receiving cash settlements and are faced for the first time with making important financial decisions on their own. Others find themselves responsible for overseeing pension funds or endowments that are of vital importance to their beneficiaries. Some have a high level of financial sophistication, but a limited amount of time to devote to their own financial affairs. Others know absolutely nothing about the world of finance, and in fact, don't have much interest in what to them is an arcane, boring, but necessary part of life.

Together we have been able to take advantage of the exciting opportunities never before available to individual investors which have exploded onto the financial landscape in the last few years. Through writing this book, I hope to show people at all levels of financial sophistication whole new ways of winning investment battles. Today, whether you are a $2,000-per-year IRA investor or a millionaire, profitable strategies once only available to the largest and most sophisticated institutional investors are within your reach. If you find yourself confronted with new and challenging investment decisions, whether you are young or old, whether you have millions to invest, or are just starting out — this book is for you.

Here you will get a basic overview of what you really need to know about stocks, bonds, and mutual funds. You will understand the role that stockbrokers play in the investment world. Professional money managers' approaches to investing will be explained. You will learn how to reach and use some of the world's best managers to build your own successful investing program.

You will also discover a new source of unbiased, non-commission-driven, investment advice. You will learn why intelligent investors are abandoning stockbrokers and turning to such advisors by the thousands. Using as examples the solutions we found to some problems and challenges various clients have faced over the years, I will show you a whole new approach to sane investing in today's confusing, and seemingly crazy, world.

As one of my friends and clients from Miami told me in his office many years ago, "My horror is of growing old and having to eat cat food on the beach." I have never forgotten that. I hope I can play a small role in helping you avoid the specter of a similar fate.

CHAPTER ONE

MONEY MAGIC YOU CAN USE

There are three great friends: an old dog, an old wife and ready money.   *— Benjamin Franklin*

Did you ever look at one of those newspaper ads for Individual Retirement Accounts (IRAs)? You know, the ones that show what a huge amount of money a twenty-one-year old will have at retirement if he or she puts away $2,000 a year until then. Did you ever see an ad for "zero coupon" bonds and wonder how you can buy a $1,000 bond maturing in 30 years so cheaply? It all seems like magic, and in a way, it is. Once you understand it, you can put the magic to work for yourself.

Albert Einstein once remarked that compound interest was one of mankinds' greatest discoveries, a true wonder of the world. Unfortunately, most of us find out about compound interest when we are too old to make it work for us.

"GENTLEMEN, MR. EINSTEIN WILL BE JOINING US TODAY IN HIS CAPACITY AS FINANCIAL WIZARD."

Ben Franklin understood compound interest. He learned about it in France from a French journalist, Mathau de la Cour. Franklin was not a terribly rich man but he was a smart man and a philanthropist at heart. In 1789, Franklin added a codicil to his will setting up two investment funds. One was established in Philadelphia, the other in Boston. The purpose was to make loans repayable at an interest rate of five percent per year to support worthy apprentices. Beginning with very small balances of about 1,000 pounds sterling (at the time approximately $4,000 - $5,000), the funds grew over the years as the loans were repaid and the interest was reinvested. By 1991, the Boston fund stood at over $4,000,000. The growth was the result of interest compounding over a very long period of time. For Franklin it was one way that a man of modest means could make a grand gift to his countrymen.

There are two cornerstone concepts of money magic — compound interest and present value. They underlie all systematic thinking about investing money.

Compound Interest

Assume that your friends Donna and Frank have a baby. To celebrate the happy event, you open a $100 savings account for the child. Assuming that the bank dutifully pays interest on the money every year, carefully reinvesting the interest payment, even at a lowly four percent interest rate, the account would grow to $331 by the child's 30th birthday. Had you invested the money in something more profitable that earned 10 percent per year after taxes, the value by the 30th birthday would have reached $1,983. The growth of the small gift is surprising in two ways: one, the compounding effect made the money grow so much. Two, there was such a huge difference in the final result between a four percent interest rate and a 10 percent interest rate. A little over twice the interest rate would have produced almost six times as much money.

It is this compounding of interest which makes it possible for us to reach retirement goals by investing money in an IRA that can grow over time without being taxed. It is this compounding of interest which also allows an insurance company to guarantee a huge death benefit to the estate of a policyholder in return for what seem to be relatively small premium payments. It is this compounding of interest which allows the small company reinvesting its earnings in its business to grow into a giant over time. It is this compounding of interest which allows a relatively small gift to a grandchild to pay for a college education eighteen years in the future. It is this compounding of interest which allowed Ben Franklin's small Boston gift to grow to over $4,000,000 more than 200 years later.

On a sour note, it is the compounding of what seems a benign three percent inflation rate which doubles our cost of living every 24 years. Since most of us will make it to our 75th birthday, we can expect the cost of living at that time to be eight times what it was when we were born. The power of the compound interest concept is perhaps better illustrated by the following table.

TABLE I

HOW $10,000 INVESTED NOW WILL GROW

(Interest Compounded Annually)

Interest rate	Years Invested				
	5	10	15	20	25
5%	12,763	16,289	20,790	26,533	33,864
8%	14,693	21,589	31,722	46,610	68,485
10%	16,105	25,937	41,772	67,275	108,347
12%	17,623	31,058	54,736	96,463	170,000
14%	19,254	37,072	71,379	137,435	264,619

Present Value

The second cornerstone concept of money magic is what is called "discounting to present value." Present value is actually the reverse of compound interest. It is more difficult to grasp than compound interest because it seems backward. Present value can be explained as the amount that one dollar coming to you at some point in your future is worth today.

Think of your childhood experience of looking through the wrong end of a telescope. Everything appeared smaller than reality, somehow magically shrunk by the lenses. Money receivable by you in the future has its worth shrunk by the time you have to wait to receive it in much the same way that the telescope shrinks optical images. If you paid a full dollar now for a future dollar, you would be foregoing the opportunity to earn interest on the money that you have in your pocket today. With that in mind, none of us would be willing to pay a dollar today, cash right out of pocket, for the guaranteed right to receive just one dollar a year from now, and certainly not ten or twenty years from now. We know intuitively that we should pay less than one dollar for that distant future dollar. If we put the dollar we have today into our savings account, we could earn a small profit on our money and it would grow over time. Maybe we could employ it at an even more profitable rate.

From Table II, we can see what $10,000 coming to us sometime in the future is worth today. The worth that we assign to that future $10,000 will depend on what investment alternatives we have available. If we feel we have alternative places to invest at 10 percent, then we are not going to be willing to pay much for that $10,000 coming to us many years in the future. If, on the other hand, our only alternative is the three percent rate being paid by our corner bank, we would be willing to pay more for the right to receive the $10,000 in the future.

If all of this is somewhat confusing, just remember that money in hand today is worth more than money coming to us tomorrow or next year. The further into the future we are going to receive money, the less it is worth to us today.

TABLE II

WHAT WOULD I PAY NOW TO GET $10,000 IN THE FUTURE

	Years in future				
	5	10	15	20	25
If I could get 10 percent elsewhere	6,209	3,855	2,394	1,486	923
If I have to settle for 3 percent at the bank	8,626	7,441	6,419	5,537	4,776

See, present value is just the reverse of compound interest.

No matter how complicated the investment problem you face, it always boils down to a basic question of what you expect to get back, when, and how much you are prepared to pay for those future rewards with today's dollars. Believe me, compound interest and present value are the cornerstone concepts of the investment world! They are money magic. Hang onto them and you can think through the most complicated investment problems.

CHAPTER TWO

WHAT CAN WE LEARN FROM MARKET HISTORY?

The best prophet of the future is the past.   — *Lord Byron*

It has been said, the main lesson we learn from history is that people don't learn from history. However, history is a good place to start when thinking about investments. Most of us tend to think in terms of investing in paper assets like stocks and bonds. Obviously, there are other investments out there like real estate, or art, or gold bars but for most of us they are impractical. Building a strip shopping center or speculating in art is not a realistic alternative for average investors. So we will stick to easily traded "paper" assets like stocks and bonds.

other investments

Accurate historical data about the rates of return on stocks and bonds in the United States is available dating back to about 1926. Two finance professors, Roger G. Ibbotson, Ph.D, and Rex A. Sinquefield, Ph.D, have compiled mountains of statistical data on the behavior of financial markets since that time. Their work has been augmented by the work of many others. Their effort is the source of the numbers you often see quoted in the financial press, accompanied by a little footnote saying, "courtesy of Ibbotson Associates." Here are the returns on various classes of stocks and bonds from 1926 through 1993 as reported by Ibbotson Associates:

TABLE III*

ANNUAL RETURNS BY ASSET CLASS 1926-1993

Stocks (small company)	+12.4%
Stocks (large company)	+10.3%
Corporate bonds (long-term)	+ 5.6%
Government bonds (long-term)	+ 5.0%
Treasury bills	+ 3.7%
Inflation	+ 3.1%

We will talk a lot more about inflation later. But for now, it is perhaps even more illuminating to look at these same returns adjusted for inflation.

TABLE IV*

ANNUAL RETURNS BY ASSET CLASS ADJUSTED FOR INFLATION
1926 — 1993

Stocks (small company)	+ 9.3%
Stocks (large company)	+ 7.2%
Corporate bonds (long-term)	+ 2.5%
Government bonds (long-term)	+ 1.9%
Treasury bills	+ .6%

*Source: *Stocks, Bonds, Bills, and Inflation 1994 Yearbook™*, Ibbotson Associates, Chicago (annually updates work by Roger G. Ibbotson and Rex A. Sinquefield). Used with permission. All rights reserved.

Clearly, stocks are the only asset class that has beaten inflation by a wide enough margin to be interesting to us.

What Is A Stock?

We use such asset return tables frequently in discussions with clients. It is not all that unusual for clients to give me a sort of sheepish blank look as though they would ask me, "What's a stock?" if they just had the nerve and were not afraid of appearing stupid. Nobody wants to look stupid. I sympathize, feeling the same reluctance to ask questions every time I visit a computer store.

A stock is nothing more than a little piece of ownership of a company. In the simplest terms, if you own a share of stock in EXXON, you actually own a tiny fraction of EXXON's cash, oil wells, ships, pipelines, executive dining room and its chairman's jet. However, because you own *so* little, don't expect to be using the company jet to fly down to Augusta for the Master's Tournament, or over to London for the Chelsea Flower Show.

If EXXON makes a profit from its operations in a given year, you as an owner, are entitled to your portion. In all probability, EXXON will pay some part of those profits out to you as a shareholder, sending you a check. The check is called a dividend. EXXON probably won't pay out all of the earnings as dividends but will, instead, reinvest some of those earnings to drill more oil wells, build more pipelines, refurbish refineries, and, perhaps, redecorate the executive dining room. Some companies don't pay cash dividends, instead plowing all of their profits back into their businesses. That's fine, so long as they can keep re-investing your money at very high rates of return. If they are successful at re-investing, your share value will grow.

Earnings Per Share (EPS) And Price Earnings (P/E) Ratios

You will often see the terms "earnings per share" and "price earnings ratios" used in discussions of stock values. Earnings per share is simply the dollar amount of the company's annual profits attributable to each share of stock. In 1993, EXXON earned $4.21 per share. At December 31, its stock price was 63 1/8 per share. The price earnings ratio is calculated by dividing the price of a share of stock at any given time by the annualized earnings attributable to that share of stock. In EXXON's case, the stock was selling at 15 times its 1993 earnings. In Wall Street parlance its price earnings ratio was 15. You will often hear that XYZ Company sells for ten times earnings or Amalgamated Behemoth Industries sells for twenty times earnings. Earnings per share and the expected growth in earnings per share is probably the single most important factor in determining what a share of the stock sells for in the market.

Remembering our lesson in discounting to present value, we can see that a share of stock is really worth the present value of its future earnings and dividends. The future earnings stream for any company is extremely difficult to forecast. It is easy to understand how different investors can have very different ideas as to a share's present value. Some, optimistic about the company's future, will think the share a bargain and want to buy. Others, pessimistic about the company's prospects are anxious to sell. It is these disagreements about value that makes stocks trade every day.

Inherited Fear Of Stocks

Looking back at historical tables of rates of return, even a bright eight-year-old would probably tell you that the answer to any investment problem is a no-brainer. "Clearly, Mom," the child would say, "we should invest all of our money in stocks!" Tables III and IV show that stocks are the only class of investment that has meaningfully outrun inflation over time. It seems that we will always be faced with the chilling prospect of ever-rising prices. At historic three percent inflation rates, what costs $1.00 today will cost $1.82 in 20 years. If inflation averages five percent, it will cost $2.71 in 20 years. Many clients and friends are providing financial support to parents who didn't understand how to guard against the inevitability of inflation during their working lifetimes.

The "all stocks" conclusion looks simple enough to that bright eight-year-old. That is because the eight-year-old hasn't yet been frightened about stocks. We adults have been told all our lives to be afraid of stocks. It was genetically imprinted on us by our parents' generation. They can either remember 1929 and the Great Depression, or they had those depression memories drilled into them, along with a fear of stocks, by our grandparents.

Diversification

There are some things about the numbers in the Ibbotson table which have to be understood. The first is that the returns on stocks represent returns on a very broadly diversified collection of stocks from literally hundreds of companies. Diversification — owning many different stocks — makes the historical market statistics work for us. Diversification is the key to successful stock investing.

Look at what happened to Marie when she suddenly became a widow in her early thirties. After her husband Jim's death, a fearful and uncertain Marie was talked into investing virtually all of her money — more than a million dollars from Jim's life insurance — in one group of limited partnership real estate ventures. The ventures were managed by a large regional real estate management company with impeccable credentials and reputation. Virtually all of Marie's investment was wiped out when commercial real estate values declined in the late 1980s. Unfortunately for Marie, she didn't heed the old saying, "Don't put all of your eggs in one basket."

Like Marie's real estate investment, any single company can fall upon hard times and its stock can either suffer a severe decline or have its value entirely wiped out. Sometimes whole groups of similar stocks can go down together when an event casts a cloud over an entire industry. When the nuclear power plant at Three Mile Island suffered its near meltdown, stocks of all the electric utility companies that had nuclear generating facilities dropped precipitously. In order for market history to work in your favor when dealing with stocks, you must be diversified. You must be sure that your investments are diverse enough that no one sour investment can hurt you enough to spoil your returns, much less wipe you out!

Stocks Are Volatile — Advances and Declines

When we say we are afraid of stocks, what we are really saying is that we are afraid of stocks' volatility. We know that stocks go up and down in value. We are afraid there may be a time when we want our money and our stocks will be down in price when we need to sell them. We can better put that risk in perspective by observing the stock market's history of advances and declines. An analysis of market history will show you that statistically the longer you hold a diversified collection of stocks, known in the investment world as a "portfolio", the less chance there is that you will suffer a loss on the stocks if one day you elect to sell them.

In investing, time is your friend. The longer your time horizon, the more advantageous it is to slant your portfolio more heavily toward stocks. One study, again drawn from the data gathered by Ibbotson, illustrates what your investment results would have been had you bought a diversified portfolio of large company stocks on the first day of any year and then liquidated that portfolio 10 years or 25 years later. Suppose you bought the stocks and hid them under your mattress for 10 years, never attempting to sell the bad investments or buy more of the good ones — a totally unmanaged stock portfolio. In 68 years you would have 58 ten-year holding periods.

During the 58 ten-year holding periods, ending December 31 of each year between 1935 and 1993, the large company stock index (your unmanaged portfolio) would have risen 56 times and fallen only two times. The two declining periods would have occurred during the Great Depression. In the 58 different 10-year periods, stocks rose faster than the rate of inflation more than 75 percent of the time. Treasury Bills beat inflation less than 50 percent of the time.

Stocks For Retirees

Often we talk with people in their fifties or early sixties about their retirement plans. Many seem to view retirement age, say 65, as a jumping-off place. They feel that on reaching their retirement day, they will be converting all of their investments into things that pay them interest like bank certificates of deposit. For some reason, they are thinking only in terms of the short time to retirement and not their very long life expectancies.

The life expectancy of a 65-year-old man is 80, so he still has at least 15 years to go. If his wife is the same age, she can expect to live another 18 years. If his wife is five years younger, her life expectancy is 22 more years. At a three percent inflation rate, her cost of living would almost double during her remaining lifetime. It doesn't make any sense for the couple to retreat to ultra-conservative investments because inflation is going to be their long-term enemy.

We began to manage some money for a delightful lady named Elizabeth when she was about eighty-years-old. Elizabeth's mother had lived to be almost one-hundred-years-old, and I have no doubt Elizabeth will match or exceed her mother's longevity. In 1970, Elizabeth became the income beneficiary of a trust managed by a large New York bank. Her husband asked the bank to invest all the trust in bonds. He was interested in increasing her income, and that strategy, at the time, would have created more monthly income than could have been expected from the dividends from a diversified portfolio of stocks. The bank as trustee refused, stating that it was bank policy to invest a minimum of at least half the trust fund in common stocks. The bank explained that they had a responsibility to protect Elizabeth's heirs from inflation. Her heirs had been designated to receive the money remaining in the trust at Elizabeth's death. Elizabeth's husband was reportedly very irritated with the bank at the time but, wherever he is now, he must be happy to know that his widow's trust is now several times larger than it would have been had it been invested as he requested. The income from the trust is much greater as well. Elizabeth's stocks, now much more valuable, have raised their dividends year after year. One day her heirs will receive a substantial inheritance.

No-Brainer Strategies

Another way of looking at the behavior of diversified stock portfolios over time is to examine a chart of the Standard & Poor's stock price index going back about 70 years. If you think of the Standard & Poor's 500 as representing the stocks of 500 of the largest U.S. companies, you will not be far wrong. Technically, the index is a little more complicated in its composition. Note that the chart describes a line which hovers around an index number of about 10 during the 1940s and 1950s.

TABLE V

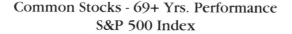

Common Stocks - 69+ Yrs. Performance
S&P 500 Index

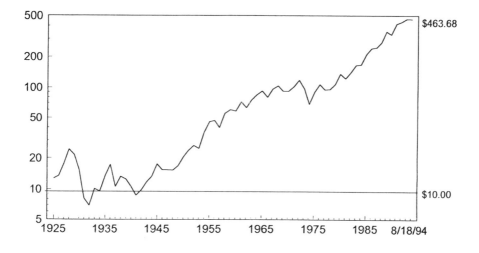

The line representing stock prices climbs erratically with a series of ups and downs until it stood at about 460 at the time this chart was prepared. If you think of it in its simplest terms, $10 invested in such a broadly diversified stock portfolio by your parents or your grandparents in those early years would have grown to $460 or to about 46 times the original investment. Not only that, the original $10 investment would be earning about $12 a year in dividends. Today's dividend income would be more than the original investment from all those years ago. The growth was the result of an unmanaged portfolio where there was never an effort made to get rid of the poor investments or add to the good ones. A "no-brainer" strategy as one of my professors used to call it.

A cautious parent or grandparent like mine, not yours I would hope, who invested money in Treasury Bills or the equivalent of today's bank savings accounts or short-term certificates of deposit, would have collected interest in small increments over all of those years, but would still have an investment worth only $10. The "no-brain" stock market investor would be 46 times as well off. From looking at the chart, it all seems so simple.

In reality, because we are real people with real brains and hard to control emotions, it is not so easy to let the favorable market statistics work for us over long time periods.

Almost everyone we talk to has had the experience of buying stocks either near or at the top of one of those bumps on the S&P 500 line. The euphoria of a rising market and the talk of easy profits tend to bring us in at near market tops. Sure enough, the market turns down, we see our money beginning to disappear, and we sell at a loss. A couple of these in-at-the-top, out-at-the-bottom, market cycles usually do the trick! Most people don't have to experience such losing efforts too many times before they conclude that stock market investing doesn't work for them. Often they abandon the idea altogether. Even a flatworm can learn a simple concept like pain avoidance. Sometimes our brains just get in the way.

Winning At Stocks Takes Patience

It is hard to be patient. Few investors are blessed with patience. That is probably why so few are successful at letting compound interest work for them. If everybody could do it, everybody would be rich by the time they were elderly.

A childhood favorite of mine, Lee Dudney, the father of one of my close friends, was a very successful businessman. He was busy and involved, and didn't spend a lot of time worrying about the stock market. For many years, every time he had a little excess money, he bought some blue chip stocks (blue chip being the term for large, well-known companies) and gave them to his wife as gifts. The

Dudneys gradually accumulated quite a widely diversified portfolio and never sold in reaction to frightening events that temporarily unsettled the market. They didn't sell when the market declined following President Eisenhower's heart attack, or when President Kennedy was assassinated, or when OPEC raised oil prices. They just held on to their stocks.

Today, many years after retiring from his business, Dudney and his wife are living comfortably off of that somewhat haphazardly put together portfolio. Whether this was an exercise in patience or the wonderful result of benign neglect, I don't know. I only know that for them the lessons of history and the statistical certainty of the benefits of stock investing have been proven.

Fear Keeps Us Out Of The Stock Market

Many of the people I talk to have no trouble intellectually grasping investment history lessons. They still have a hard time bringing themselves to make the plunge into buying a diversified stock portfolio. Events surrounding us, reported in the newspapers and on television, make us feel anxious about the future.

Psychologically, it can be difficult to get up the courage to enter the stock market in any meaningful way. William, one of my older and wiser acquaintances, recalls attending a college course on investments shortly after WWII. He fondly remembers his professor explaining to the class that the most difficult time to make an investment, a time filled with uncertainty and doubts about the future, is whenever you have the money.

Market Timing

It is always tempting to think that we are smart enough to figure out the direction of the next little bump in that line on the Standard & Poor's chart. Most of the rhetoric in the popular financial press is generated by people telling you that the market is going to go up and therefore you should buy, or down and therefore you should sell, avoiding the coming catastrophe. I have observed a lot of these "market timers" over the years. I don't know any who have become rich based on their market timing.

On April 23, 1990, *The Dick Davis Digest* published an article on chaos theory and the futility of trying to time one's buying and selling as it relates to the stock market.

> Capital appreciation doesn't come in even steps - but typically in intense bursts of activity. You would have to be in the market, as well as out, at just the right time. A dollar invested in stocks in January of 1980 would have grown to five dollars by the end of 1989. If your market timing efforts left you out of the market in the best five months—, just four percent of the total time—, your dollar would have grown to only $2.90, not much more than the $2.35 you would have had by just staying in Treasury Bills. That's why we say market timing is a losing game. So the next time you are frustrated over the difficulty in calling the market's ups and downs, consider this: chaos theory says it is not possible; historical studies show it is not even necessary.

In another study, noted by Burt Berry in his **NoLOAD Fund *X* newsletter, Woodside Asset Management did a detailed analysis of the big 1982-1987 bull (rising) market which lasted 1,276 trading days. The S&P 500 averaged annual returns including dividends of 26 percent over this period. If you had been out of the market for only the top 10 trading days, your annual return dropped to 18 percent from 26 percent. If you missed the top 20 days, the return dropped to 13 percent. If you were out for the best 40 days, the return dropped to 4 percent.

"DR. FERNWOOD HERE IS A PROPONENT OF THE THEORY THAT YOU CAN PREDICT THE ACTIVITY OF THE STOCK MARKET BY THE BEHAVIOR OF WOOLY WORMS."

More recently, in 1991, the Standard & Poor's 500 Index was up more than 30 percent. If you had been out of the market for just 21 days from 1/14/91 through 1/31/91, and from 12/20/91 through 12/31/91, your return would have dropped from 30 percent to about nine percent. Big gains come in short unpredictable spurts. You can't really expect to move that fast.

Picking The Worst Time To Invest

Investors always have a fear of coming in "at the top". Frank A. Jones, a Registered Investment Adviser, wrote a column in *The Commercial Appeal* newspaper of Memphis, Tennessee, which included a table showing the results of investing $5,000 at the peak of the market every year for 20 years beginning in 1973. To do that, you would have had to be a profoundly unlucky investor picking the very worst day of each year to put your money to work. Here is his table:

TABLE VI

20 YEARS OF PEAK INVESTING

The result of investing $5,000 at the peak of the market every year for 20 years beginning in 1973.

Date of Market High	Cumulative Investment	Value of Account on 12/31*
1/11/73	5,000	4,189
1/03/74	10,000	6,688
7/15/75	15,000	13,990
9/21/76	20,000	22,404
1/03/77	25,000	25,455
9/12/78	30,000	31,725
10/05/79	35,000	42,796
11/28/80	40,000	61,170
1/06/81	45,000	62,860
11/09/82	50,000	81,353
10/10/83	55,000	104,453
11/06/84	60,000	115,913
12/16/85	65,000	157,622
12/02/86	70,000	191,773
8/25/87	75,000	205,496
10/21/88	80,000	244,336
10/09/89	85,000	326,471
7/16/90	90,000	320,885
12/31/91	95,000	423,189
12/18/92	100,000	460,356

* based on Standard & Poor's 500 Index

How Do I Get Income From My Stock Portfolio?

Logically, you might wonder how you can begin to use a stock investment portfolio to produce a steady income stream. After all, stocks go up and down and the dividends might not be enough to cover the annual need for income.

Using the example above, suppose our unlucky investor who always picked the worst day of the year to buy stocks had retired in 1982 and instead of investing money each year thereafter decided to take $5,000 a year out of his stock portfolio. He began withdrawals at the end of 1982 leaving the balance invested in stocks.

Year ended 12/31	Value of Account	Withdrawal
1983	88,532	5,000
1984	89,021	5,000
1985	112,152	5,000
1986	128,012	5,000
1987	129,669	5,000
1988	146,064	5,000
1989	187,220	5,000
1990	176,416	5,000
1991	225,046	5,000
1992	237,149	5,000
1993	256,101	5,000

Our unlucky investor did suffer some volatility. The account actually dropped in value in 1990, and made very little money in both 1984 and 1987. By now, the annual income taken from the account could have been increased substantially had the investor wished to withdraw more money. The account benefitted from stock price appreciation as well as dividends. Our retiree didn't care where his money came from. If he didn't have enough dividend income every year, he simply sold enough stock to make up the difference and then withdrew $5,000 from the account. Maybe he wasn't so unlucky after all.

Dollar Cost Averaging vs. Investing It All Now

Over the years, you may have read about a technique called "dollar cost averaging". Dollar cost averaging is a popular and widely recommended technique in which you put the same amount of money into the market or into a single stock or a mutual fund at regular time intervals. The tables above are a good example of dollar cost averaging and systematic withdrawals, except they are a little different since money was put in on the worst day of each year rather than at regular time intervals. The idea of dollar cost averaging is to make your investments in the same dollar amounts month after month or year after year. If you do you will accumulate more shares when the market is down because you can buy them cheaply, and fewer shares when the market is high and shares are more expensive.

Theoretically, and over a long period of time, this method does somewhat reduce risk but, according to a study by two finance professors at Wright State University in Dayton, Ohio, reported in *Investor's Business Daily* on January 10, 1994, this method produces lower returns than putting your money to work all at once.

"The stock market has an upward bias," said Wright State finance professor Peter Bacon who performed the study with Richard Williams, associate dean of business at Wright State. "Generally speaking," said Bacon, "you are just better off being in." The article said that the study's results can be applied most easily to investors who come into sudden money through inheritances, bonuses, lottery winnings or asset sales and don't know what to do with lump sums.

Implicit in the study is the belief that as Bacon noted, "nobody knows when the market is going to go up or down."

So Bacon and Williams demonstrate that it's better to have all of your money working for you in the market as soon as you can if you are investing for five years or more. You need to have a reasonably long time frame because there is always the chance that the market will go down as soon as you invest and you will need time for the market's upward bias to work in your favor.

Bacon and Williams further suggested that if you were going to make a lump-sum investment in the market, you should always diversify. They suggested putting some money in foreign stocks, some in small company stocks, some in growth stocks, and some in underpriced "value" stocks. Also they advised that you keep your money in for at least five years and avoid reading the financial tables in the newspapers on a daily basis. "Get your money in when you get the money, and then keep focused on the long term."

In a 1991 article by P.R. Chandy and William Reichenstein, entitled "Timing Strategies and the Risk of Missing Bull Markets", the timing dilemma was described in very real terms. The authors noted,

> ...the plight of Wall Street's highest-paid professionals during the four-week market surge that began in January, 1991 demonstrates the difficulty of market timing. Strategists at Goldman Sachs, Merrill Lynch, Morgan Stanley, and Salomon Brothers predicted a continuation of the bear market. They were not alone. Randall Smith of *The Wall Street Journal* reported that at the beginning of the Middle East war with Iraq, only 35 percent of investment advisors were predicting a rising market. This episode illustrates a consistent finding in market research: The pro's crystal ball is at best opaque. As a group, prediction performance of the pros is decidedly average. Simply put, market timing is risky and no one can predict the stock market with anything approaching certainty.

Martin came to us in early January of 1991 with several hundred thousand dollars. It was available for long term investment. Martin was a great believer in stocks. He was concerned, however, that if war broke out after Iraq's invasion of Kuwait the stock market would take a major tumble. To no avail we tried to convince him that because that perception was so widely held, just the opposite might occur. To hedge his bet, we suggested the immediate investment of half his money. The balance could be put to work when and if the war broke out. Martin was adamant in his refusal. He was sure the stock market would drop like a stone when the first shot was fired. Everybody said so! It was going to be the greatest buying opportunity in history!

The morning following the beginning of Operation Desert Storm, the stock market took off like a rocket. The Dow Jones Industrial Average was up around 100 points. An excited Martin called asking if we had put his money to work before the event as I had suggested. I assured him that we would never do such a thing without his permission. "What a great way to get sued!", I told him. He chewed me out good-naturedly and admitted, "That's the reason I need a money manager."

Why Do Stocks Rise Over Time?

All these references to statistical market history can seem a little hypothetical. "History is one thing, but how do I know this rising stock market will keep going? Every day my morning paper says the market is going down and stocks are not good investments," you might say. Fortunately, in the real world there are reasons why stock prices, in the aggregate, rise over time. It's not over!

Compound interest works for companies just as it works in investor portfolios or savings accounts. If you own shares of stock in a company that has a good business, sells a good product, and is growing over time with the country's population and the markets, your company probably will earn a yearly profit and share part of it with you through dividend checks. The rest of the company's earnings will be re-invested in its business where those invested dollars should be expected to earn a reasonable return. This year-in and year-out plowing back and re-investing of earnings ultimately takes a small company and turns it into a big one. As a shareholder the value of the assets that you own, represented by your shares of stock, continues to grow. The value of your shares of stock should increase as well.

Inflation also plays a significant role in explaining these rising earnings streams. Inflation has been with us for a long time. Some of us can remember the three-cent stamp, the nickel Coca-Cola and the thirty-cent gallon of gas. The new 1964 1/2 Ford Mustang convertible, for which I saddled myself with an unbearable debt burden of about $2,500 was a triumph of emotion over logic. It was dark blue, fast, and had a white top - irresistible. A new Mustang convertible today, some thirty years later, sells for more than $20,000!

Consider the effect of inflation on a company's earnings. Think of a chewing gum manufacturer in the 1950s selling his product for a nickel, perhaps earning a fraction of a penny per pack. All these years later the same product, manufactured by virtually the same technology, sells for a quarter per pack. That penny per pack earned years ago has probably grown into many pennies per pack today. Assuming you were a shareholder of the chewing gum company during that entire time period, you would have seen a dramatic increase in the earnings attributable to your shares of stock. All things being equal, you should have had a corresponding increase in the value of your shares.

Holding On In Frightening Times

In spite of all of this logical support for the concept of long-term investing in the stock market, if you are like most people you still find it frightening. The market goes up and down, the newspapers are full of frightening news and we carry the genetic imprint from our parents and grandparents that bonds are safer.

I ran across a quote from Bill Berger in a recent annual report summarizing the performance of his Berger 100 and Berger 101 mutual funds. Bill's funds have been very successful over the years and he is clearly a knowledgeable investor. I thought it particularly telling that he recognized one of his greatest contributions was simply keeping his investors in the market long enough to let market forces work in their favor.

SIRE, EVERY TIME YOU START TALKING ABOUT PILLAGING AND BURNING, THE STOCK MARKET GOES CRAZY!"

In his president's letter, Bill wrote, "Our mission is to serve as the active investment partner of those who have the gumption to save for their future and who have the foresight to stick with it when everyone else is in a state of doubt or even panic."

It is not always easy to keep people in the market when they are frightened. A prominent dentist who had invested some of his wife's inheritance in a portfolio of stocks panicked when the presidential election results of 1992 were known. He sold all of her stocks assuming that the market would tumble. The presidential results had been broadly anticipated by investors who had pushed the market to lower levels in the months preceding the election. Once the uncertainty was cleared up, the market began what turned out to be a substantial and long-running advance.

We are all unnerved by market-shaking occurrences such as a military invasion or political disruptions. It is hard to realize that often they are fleeting events, and not permanent changes likely to affect the entire course of human history. The market usually bounces back from them within a few months. The key is to put them in their proper perspective. Ask yourself, "Is this really likely to affect the value of large companies five years from now?" If the answer is no, grit your teeth and ride out the storm. The truly courageous use these times as buying opportunities.

"All of this sounds great," you are probably saying, "but, how come in real life, people like me have such a hard time picking stocks and making money in the market?"

CHAPTER THREE

WHY IS PICKING STOCKS SO HARD?

I don't like money, actually, but it quiets my nerves.

— *Joe Louis*

We all hear talk about the stock market. We may be at the office, on an airplane, at a cocktail party, or maybe even attending a PTA meeting. From time to time, we are regaled with tales of investment success. Stories are bandied about in the surgeons' lounge, on the golf course, at garden club meetings, or during acrobics class. When we hear about these successes we say to ourselves, "It seems so common to get these doubles and triples, so why do I find it so hard? Why can't I do it?"

It Really Is Hard

Don't feel bad or alone. It really is difficult to pick stocks that double and triple in any given year. The following table analyzes two very good years in the United States' stock market. In both years, a diversified portfolio of stocks that equaled the market's performance would have done very well, rising over 20 percent. Notice the percentage of stocks that would have doubled or tripled during the year:

TABLE VII

Two Very Good Years for Investors
In New York Stock Exchange Listed Stocks

	1982	1983
Percentage of stocks gaining	70.0%	79.0%
Percentage of stocks doubling	5.6%	5.1%
Percentage of stocks tripling	0.7%	0.5%

Surprise! Even in a good year only approximately five percent of all the stocks on the New York Stock Exchange double in price. That means you would have had to buy at least twenty randomly selected stocks to have a chance at getting a double. You would have had to buy almost two-hundred stocks in a great year to get a triple. Now maybe you don't feel so badly! Remember, people who assault you with their tales of doubles and triples are probably reluctant to tell you about the losers they've owned. That is human nature.

It Is Hard Even If You Know The Chairman

Not only is it statistically difficult to pick big winners, but there are other more subtle reasons why stock investing is difficult. One of the justifications for buying stocks which I frequently hear goes something like this. "It is a local company, they are doing well, and they are very busy. I know that because my brother-in-law works there. He told me that they are going to split the stock." Even better than that, and the ultimate clincher is, "I know the chairman, he's my next door neighbor, and he says it is a great company."

In my earlier career, I spent some years as chairman of one small, lackluster, and somewhat troubled New York Stock Exchange-listed company. Most of my time was spent trying to keep the company solvent by selling off some divisions and refinancing others. It would have been more fun to have been chairman of GE but you don't get those jobs at 35. Simultaneously, I served for a time as chief financial officer and a director of a Fortune 500 company also listed on the New York Stock Exchange that was a major manufacturer of building materials. During those years, I had the unique opportunity for a young man of being one of the people in the business charged with giving information about our activities to investors, the press, our employees, and lenders.

Information From Companies Is "Rosy"

All top executives of large public companies are confronted with the same public relations problems. They have to be careful what they say publicly. It falls upon the executive's shoulders to try to keep lenders comfortable with their loans, employees feeling good about their prospects for continued employment, and shareholders enthusiastic about the company's prospects.

Most, but not all, executives are honest. For some, with so much money at risk, there is a temptation to issue press releases that are overly optimistic. Others will use aggressive accounting to inflate reported earnings. Accounting trickery is not always easy for auditors to recognize and, sometimes, it takes several years for real problems to surface. Fortunately, such cases are rare.

I can assure you that most corporate executives don't lie to the press. When *The Wall Street Journal* calls, you are going to tell them the truth. But there is a natural tendency to put as positive a spin on any corporate story as possible. In any business, there are always things to worry about. Business is trouble! Still, unless the worrisome things are very likely to happen, they are probably not going to make it into the news. As a reader, you don't really ever find out about the business concerns that may awaken the chairman in the middle of the night with that chilling feeling. Every executive has these.

There are some other more subtle influences on the company's executives. Everybody likes to feel proud of what they do and good about the organization they are involved with. Like grandparents displaying pictures of their grandchildren, executives tend to emphasize the virtues of their companies and downplay their shortcomings.

Company Executives Like High Stock Prices

It is likely that the top executives of a company either own a lot of the company's stock or have a right to buy a lot of the stock cheaply under stock option plans. They are vitally interested in getting their stock price up and keeping it high. In many cases, the stock represents most of their personal worth. Why do you think large corporations hire financial public relations firms?

The Media and Pop Finance

Most of us don't have direct access to company managements. We are forced to rely on what we read in newspapers or magazines, or see on television.

Recently, I was talking with one of our clients, a physician, about the poor quality of financial information sometimes reported in the news media. It is not unusual on the day following one of these stories, usually the ones predicting the end of the world and the demise of financial markets as we know them, to have clients call worried sick about their investments. He explained that in his medical practice, he encountered a similar phenomenon. Patients suddenly recognize their aches and pains match the symptoms associated with the dread disease they have just read or heard about. They immediately call his office sure that they are afflicted with that very malady. The doctor calls it "pop medicine". In our industry, we call the similar phenomenon "pop finance".

Pop finance has many roots. You will read or hear wonderfully favorable news reports about companies that have been planted with a gullible reporter. The source of these stories is usually a speculator who has a fistful of the stock. He hopes that the story will push the stock price up. If it works, the speculator can unload his shares at a high price. This is a technique known as "buy first, promote later".

Even more insidious are articles and rumors planted by people who are "short." Short means that you are making a bet that the stock price is going to fall. If it does, you stand to make a handsome profit. If a major national publication can be encouraged to publish a negative story about a company, particularly one that is selling at a high price relative to its earnings, you can be sure the price will drop dramatically when the article appears. These negative stories appear in one of the nation's most respected weekly financial publications with monotonous regularity. You are indeed unlucky if your stock becomes the "victim of the week." Truth matters in the long run but not in the short run. Investors sell first and ask questions later.

How About Financial Newsletters?

A few financial newsletters are thoughtful and written by responsible people with something to say. There are several of these listed in Appendix C. However, the vast majority of financial newsletters issue opinions that are useless to the serious investor.

Years ago I was introduced to a stock market newsletter writer in Miami. The writer was well-known and quoted from time to time by the national press. He was occasionally interviewed on television. I felt I was in the presence of a celebrity. Over lunch, we discussed the stock market and some stocks in particular. When asked why he never seemed to write negative articles either on the market or on companies, he told me that while he might feel negative, negative newsletters don't sell! He was in the newsletter business, not the business of managing money. If his newsletter did not sell and his subscription base did not grow, he could not survive financially. I was stunned by his comments.

This particular media star later decided to try his hand at managing money for clients. Their portfolios performed even worse than his newsletter recommendations had done. Happily for investors, he has since disappeared from public view.

Sometimes A Company's Results Are Not Reflected In Its Stock Price

Further complicating the successful picking of individual stocks is the effect of outside influences such as the Three Mile Island incident which depressed nuclear utility stocks in 1979. Academics have tried for years to isolate the relative importance of what goes on within a company and the effect that has on its share price, from outside events that can also affect share prices. Various studies indicate as much as 80 percent of what happens to a company's stock price has nothing whatsoever to do with what is currently going on within the company. Other studies come up with somewhat lower percentages but almost anyone who is a student of the financial markets would agree that at least half the factors affecting stock prices are forces outside the company.

Diligently doing your homework on a company, understanding its financial statements and its business, holding the management in high regard, and believing the underlying truth of the information flowing from the company are all important in selecting stocks. None of that insulates you from the unexpected and out-of-the-blue impact of say, a Mid-East conflict that threatens the world's oil supplies. Regardless of the quality of your homework, if fear drives the stock market down 20 percent, your stocks are probably going to go down temporarily too.

" SAY, HOW MUCH STOCK DID YOU SAY YOU HAD IN THAT RUNNING SHOE COMPANY?"

Outside influences don't have to be as dramatic as an invasion that unsettles the whole market. Individual stocks can be influenced by more narrowly focused events. The Federal Reserve can raise or lower interest rates. International currency values can change, altering earnings prospects for large multi-national companies. OPEC can cut oil production driving up energy prices. Politicians may decide it would be politically popular to criticize a particular industry like health care, putting the stocks of medically related companies under a cloud.

Investor psychology can have a similar effect. Investors seem to have a herd mentality. One year they may fall in love with the stocks of running shoe companies; a year later running shoe companies' stocks will have fallen dramatically from their previous highs as casino gambling issues capture the public's attention.

John Maynard Keynes, who many regard as the most influential 20th century economist, was also a very successful stock market speculator. Writing in 1910, Keynes said, "The investor will be affected, as is obvious, not by the net income he will actually receive from his investment in the long run, but by his expectations. These will often depend upon fashion, upon advertisement, or upon purely irrational waves of optimism or depression."

Clearly, in picking stocks we have a lot of things to think about that go beyond just knowing the company. Stephen A. Ross, Professor of Economics and Finance at Yale's School of Organization and Management, said in *The Wall Street Journal* in August, 1988, "It doesn't do much good to know the price/earnings ratios or the capitalization of a stock unless you know how those characteristics relate to the behavior of financial markets." He added that all any investment strategy really does is provide a recipe for building a portfolio that has a specific set of economic sensitivities or "factor bets." These factors include such things as inflation, interest rates, commodity prices, capital spending and investor confidence. No wonder stock picking is so tough!

CHAPTER FOUR

I FEEL SAFER WITH BONDS, I UNDERSTAND THEM . . . I THINK

I have enough money to last the rest of my life, unless I buy something.
　　　　　　　　　　　　　　　　　　　　— Jackie Mason

Bonds should be easier to understand and deal with than stocks. A bond is a pretty simple animal, nothing more than a piece of paper representing a promise to pay back some money that some government entity or company has borrowed. The bond specifies an interest rate and when interest payments will be made. That rate is what the borrower is willing to pay the bond holder for the use of the money until it is repaid. The day the money is scheduled to be paid back to the bond holder is referred to as the maturity date. Unlike a stock, where future earnings, dividends, and the selling price are uncertain, cash flows from a bond are more certain. It's easier to think about in discounted present value terms.

Usually the more distant the bond's maturity date — that is, the longer we lend our money — the higher interest rate we can expect to receive. The graph in Table VIII depicts a "normal" yield curve for U.S. Treasury securities. You can see that if we loan the government money for very short periods like 30 days, 90 days, or a year, they pay us lower rates of interest than they would if we loaned them money for 30 years. Occasionally when money is very tight (scarce), short-term rates will exceed long-term rates. The result is what is known as an "inverted" yield curve and usually precedes a recession. If you want to impress someone ask them what they think the shape of the yield curve will be in the next six months to a year. They will think you are a bond expert.

TABLE VIII
U.S. TREASURY YIELD CURVE

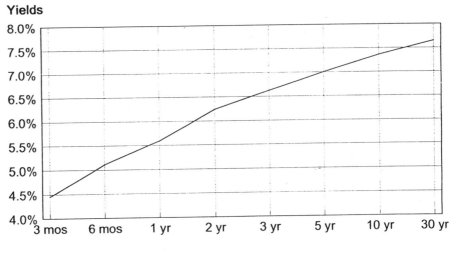

Maturities

Bond Buyers Don't Get Rich

We've already discovered that stocks have outperformed all other types of investments over time. We also learned that corporate and government bonds historically have kept only slightly ahead of inflation. In all my years of studying financial markets, I have never heard of anyone who ever made a large fortune buying and holding bonds. I have never seen a hospital wing donated by someone who made a fortune owning bonds. It may be possible to find hospital wings donated by bond sales people, bond speculators, and bond dealers, but not bond buyers. One of my more successful clients who used to be in the bond business once remarked, "bonds are to be sold, not bought!"

I don't intend to imply that there is no place for bonds in an investor's portfolio. Many people, however, buy bonds or are sold bonds because of their assumed safety without really understanding the potential pitfalls. We will explore some of those pitfalls as we learn about bonds.

Simple Kinds Of Bonds — U.S. Treasury

The easiest kind of bond to understand is a good old United States Treasury Bond. Treasury bonds can be bought in $1,000 denominations. If you buy a new bond, you are, in effect, loaning $1,000 to the United States government. If your new bond has a twenty-year maturity, the government will pay you interest on your money every six months for twenty years and then send you back your $1,000. Bonds are sold by the government to come due (mature) at various times in the future from a very few years on up to about thirty years. Technically, bonds sold by the Treasury that mature in more than one but less than 10 years are called Treasury Notes. Treasury Bills mature in one year or less.

Like the government, corporations, cities and states, and even churches will borrow money from time to time by issuing bonds. All sorts of different gimmicks and features are sometimes included in bonds to try to make them easier to sell to the public or to give the borrowers certain advantages.

Investors who buy bonds which are direct obligations of the U.S. government, or those that are guaranteed by the U.S. government, often feel that they are taking the safest possible course of action. They know that the United States government will stand by its obligations and make the interest and principal payments on time even if the government has to print new money to do it. Buying a twenty- or thirty-year government bond can seem like a pretty good idea to someone who plans to put the bond away for a very long length of time. "At least", they think to themselves, "I'll get all my money back when the bond comes due." The buyer probably never learned our discounted present value lesson. If he had, he wouldn't place much value on receiving $1,000 thirty years in the future when the bond matures. Even at a three percent inflation rate, the purchasing power of that $1,000 will shrink to about $407.

Bonds And Inflation

David Dreman writing in *Forbes Magazine* pointed out that if an investor had plunked down $100,000 in 1946 for long-term government bonds, he would have had $25,000 in purchasing power left at the end of 1988, some 43 years later. After taxes and inflation, the investment would have declined 75 percent.

As investors, inflation is our most insidious and intractable enemy. In spite of recession and monetary restraint by the United States Federal Reserve Bank, inflation seems to be a continuing, nagging problem for the U.S. economy. Today we speak of 3 percent inflation as almost acceptable or normal, a level that, viewed from the 1950s or 1960s, would have been horrifying.

Interest Rate Risk — I Need To Sell My Bonds

Beyond the inflation risk, there is what is known as interest rate risk. Real people, like you and me, seldom can be very certain about where we are going to be and what we are going to be doing in 10, 20, or 30 years. Think back 10, 20, or 30 years. Could you have predicted with any accuracy where you are and what you are doing today? I could not.

It is not at all unusual for the owner of a bond to decide within a few years after purchasing it that he has some alternative need for

the money. Many people have sold bonds they thought they would hold forever to help their children buy a house or perhaps finance a business. That sort of unexpected need for money happens all the time.

Unsophisticated investors who buy long-term government bonds because of their safety may learn the hard way that they may not be able to sell the bond for what they paid for it if they need to sell it before maturity. If interest rates in the real world change after they buy the bond, its market value will either be higher or lower than the original cost.

The Interest Rate Seesaw

Think of bond prices and interest rates as though they are the names of two children playing on the seesaw at the schoolyard. The little red-haired boy with "bond price" written on his t-shirt is going to move down when the little blond girl with pigtails in the pinafore [sleeveless dress or apron] with "interest rate" embroidered on it rides her end of the seesaw upwards. If interest rates go up, bond prices go down and vice-versa.

There is more to the seesaw illustration than first meets the eye. If our little boy "bond price" is sitting pretty close to the middle of the seesaw, he won't go too far up or down as the little girl rises and falls. If he finds himself, however, way out at the end of the seesaw, he will go up and down in a wide arc. Think of the length of his side of the seesaw as representing years to maturity with one being near the center and 30 being way out at the end. A bond with many years to go before it matures, say thirty, will be very sensitive to changes in interest rates. Its market value can move up and down over a very wide range. It has not been unusual in recent history for the prices of these absolutely safe United States Treasury Bonds to exhibit more price volatility than the stock market.

TABLE IX

How Changes In Interest Rates
Affect Bond Prices
Assuming a $1,000 Bond Paying Eight Percent Interest

IF RATES
RISE ONE PERCENT

Bond Maturity	Market Value	Percentage Change
2 YEARS (Short-Term)	$982	-1.8%
5 YEARS (Intermediate-Term)	$960	-4.0%
20 YEARS (Long-Term)	$908	-9.2%

IF RATES
FALL ONE PERCENT

Bond Maturity	Market Value	Percentage Change
2 YEARS (Short-Term)	$1,018	+1.8%
5 YEARS (Intermediate-Term)	$1,042	+4.2%
20 YEARS (Long-Term)	$1,107	+10.7%

The Concept Of Total Return

When you think about buying a bond you should always think about total return, not just interest rates. Total return takes changes in bond values, as well as interest rates, into consideration. Suppose you bought a bond yielding six percent for $1,000. If you sold it a year later for $960, you would have earned $60 in interest but lost $40 on the sale. Your profit from the whole transaction would have been only $20, or two percent. Your total return would have been two percent. Say your bond price had gone up rather than down in a year. If you could sell the bond at the end of that year for $1,040 your total return would have been the $60 in interest plus the $40 profit on the sale for a total return of $100 or 10 percent. This shows how much changes in bond prices can affect total return.

Zero Coupon Bonds

Zero coupon bonds are often sold to investors with the idea that you put up a very little bit of money today to get back a big chunk in the future (remember compound interest). Zero coupon bonds are much more volatile than regular interest bearing bonds. Zeros, as they are called, are about three times as volatile as regular interest-paying bonds and make wonderful speculative instruments for playing the interest rate markets. They can be devastatingly poor investments if you are forced to liquidate them at a time when interest rates have moved up. If your zeros are not held in a non-taxable account, like an IRA or a profit sharing trust, you have to pay the tax on the small annual increases in value as the bonds age towards maturity. That is a bad deal as the bond produces no cash interest payments but you have to send a check for your taxes to the government anyway.

Beyond Treasuries — Credit Risk

When you venture into other kinds of bonds and away from United States government Bonds, you begin to encounter another kind of risk — credit risk. That is the kind of risk you take when you loan your brother-in-law money to invest in his latest sure-fire winner: a tropical fish emporium franchise in Dubuque. You may or may not get your money back. I experienced the same kind of risk when I advanced my son David, then a nine-year-old, one dollar to be paid back out of his three-dollar weekly allowance. I am still waiting. As I write this, David is 21.

Because credit risk is such an important issue, and because not all investors have the financial sophistication to properly evaluate the long-term interest-paying ability of the companies, states, cities or towns — much less foreign governments that issue bonds — a mini-industry of credit rating agencies exists. The two best-known are Moody's and Standard & Poor's. Each rates bonds based on credit worthiness. A sample of the Standard & Poor's ratings is included in Appendix A.

credit rating agencies

Risk Of Call

Another risk and one that has become much more meaningful to investors in recent years as interest rates have trended downward, is the risk of "call". A call is simply a provision that says the borrower may pay the bond off early if the borrower wishes. While United States Treasury bonds are generally not callable, most other bonds both corporate and municipal (tax-free) have call provisions. Borrowers like being able to pay bonds off early in the event that interest rates fall. The call provision is the right of the borrower to go somewhere else and borrow the money cheaper, and then use it to pay off the original bond holder. It is similar to re-financing your home mortgage, paying off your old loan at one bank, using a new, cheaper loan from another bank.

Many of our clients who bought bonds five or ten years ago when interest rates were much higher than they are today, have had their bonds paid off early. What do you do when all of those wonderful 10 or 12 percent tax-free municipal bonds, which you thought you were going to be able to hold for 20 years, are repaid early and you end up sitting with cash that can only be invested at five, six, or seven percent?

Sometimes Bonds Make Sense In Portfolios

While I am not a great fan of bonds as permanent investments for long-term investors, I am well aware that they have a definite place in some investors' portfolios. You probably remember our eighty-year-old client, Elizabeth. Well, she had some other money in addition to her trust. We used it to build a portfolio to provide her with income from bonds and some inflation protection from stocks. We constructed the portfolio with a mix of 75 percent bonds and 25 percent stocks. Elizabeth has definite income needs that can be met by the bonds' periodic interest payments and, at her age, she doesn't feel comfortable assuming the volatility risk of an all-stock portfolio.

You will run across similar situations if you are ever cast in a fiduciary (responsible for other people's money) role. Many people, at one time or another, serve on the boards of charitable institutions where they have responsibility for endowment funds or are trustees of employee pension plans. Many choose investment portfolio mixes that balance stocks and bonds in roughly equal proportions. Their objective is the same as Elizabeth's. They want to dampen out some of the volatile swings that an all-stock portfolio might experience.

The following table explains the effect of different mixes of stocks and bonds on total portfolio returns over time. It also illustrates risk as measured by downside volatility. For instance, if you pick out a mix of 70 percent stocks and 30 percent bonds from the left column on the table, you can see that the worst year you would have had was a -17 percent and the best a +39 percent. Your average return over the 1947-1989 study would have been +11 percent. You will find the results of other combinations spelled out in Table X:

TABLE X
TOTAL PORTFOLIO RETURNS OVER TIME

If you own	Single largest one-year loss	Your average return*	Single largest one-year gain
100% stocks** No bonds ***	-26.5%	+13.5%	+52.6%
90% stocks 10% bonds	-23.4%	+12.7%	+48.1%
80% stocks 20% bonds	-20.3%	+11.8%	+43.5%
70% stocks 30% bonds	-17.2%	+11.0%	+39.0%
60% stocks 40% bonds	-14.4%	+10.1%	+34.4%
50% stocks 50% bonds	-11.1%	+ 9.3%	+31.6%
40% stocks 60% bonds	- 8.0%	+ 8.4%	+32.8%
30% stocks 70% bonds	- 6.1%	+ 7.6%	+34.7%
20% stocks 80% bonds	- 5.8%	+ 6.7%	+36.6%
10% stocks 90% bonds	- 5.9%	+ 5.9%	+38.5%
No stocks 100% bonds	- 9.2%	+ 5.0%	+40.4%

*From 1947-1989, compounded annually, dividends re-invested
**Measured by Standard & Poor's 500
***Long-term U.S. Treasury Bonds

Sources: Towneley Capital Management, New York; Standard & Poor's Corporation; Ibbotson Associates; Crandall, Pierce and Company.

Using the data contained in this table, the trustees of a medium-size company established a profit sharing plan to meet the retirement needs of a great number of production workers and a few executives. While the trustees of the plan, who are also executives in the company, understand that they would make more money in the long run if all of the plan assets were invested in common stocks, they have chosen to give up some of the higher expected returns that such a strategy would generate. Bonds have been included in the portfolio in the hope that at the end of any given year, their financially unsophisticated workers, particularly those nearing retirement, would not be alarmed or have their plans disrupted by a sharp stock market sell-off which could cause a decline in their retirement accounts.

Short Maturity Bonds For "Parking" Cash

Short maturity bonds are a good place to "park" money. If you have a specific use for money, such as building a house or sending a child to college in two or three years, short maturity bonds will generally provide you with better interest rates than bank savings accounts or CDs.

No one can really determine the near-term direction of the stock market. Stock investments should usually be avoided for short duration investments, those of fewer than five years.

Traps For Bond Buyers

As in any area of the financial markets, bond buyers need to be aware of the pitfalls that exist. Bonds are frequently packaged by brokerage houses into products like Unit Trusts and Closed-End Bond Funds. Beware of both!

The Unit Trust Trap

A Unit Trust is most frequently a big basket of tax-free municipal bonds from a number of different issuers, put together by a brokerage house and then carved into little pieces for sale by stockbrokers. For $1,000 you can buy one unit, which represents a small part of this highly diversified bond portfolio. Generally, these portfolios are not managed once they are established. The bonds are put into the hands of a trustee whose only obligation is to act on behalf of the unit holders in case of a default. They are not expected to sell bonds if they think an issuer's credit is going bad, nor are they expected to trade the bonds to improve yields or credit quality for you, the unit holder.

Most of these baskets of bonds are put together by John Nuveen & Co., Van Kampen Merritt, or a syndicate of brokers led by Merrill Lynch. The brokers usually mix a lot of bonds that have high interest payment rates with others giving more normal rates. That way they can make the resulting average interest rate on the units attractive to us as potential unit buyers. There is a general suspicion among knowledgeable investors that many of the bonds used in these packages are those that would be difficult for the bond dealers to sell otherwise. Could it be that this packaging of bonds for sale to small investors is a great way to get rid of stale bond inventory?

Unit trusts are too often a heads-you-lose, tails-you-lose investment. If interest rates rise they fall in market value like any other bond. You would expect them to rise as interest rates fall, but often they don't. Remember what happens to high-interest-rate bonds when interest rates fall. The stronger borrowers call in their old bonds and pay off the unit trust. We unit holders wind up getting cash back and holding units in a diminished trust that is left with only low-interest-rate-bearing bonds or those issued by the weaker credits. Where we normally would have expected as bond buyers to benefit from falling interest rates (remember the seesaw), instead we have been tricked.

The Closed-End Bond Fund Trap

Closed-end bond funds are somewhat like unit trusts in that they are large pools of bonds. The difference is that closed-end funds are under active management. Unlike the unit trusts, the closed-end fund managers are expected to buy and sell bonds and make money for us. A brokerage firm puts together a pool of bonds, say $100,000,000 worth or more, and then sells shares of the pool to the public. They frequently trade on exchanges like The New York Stock Exchange. When the pools are put together and the shares are sold as new issues, the brokerage firms generally get about seven percent of our money to cover the expense of putting the pool together and paying commissions to stockbrokers who sell the shares to investors. Frequently, once the shares are sold to investors like you and me, they drift down in value, reflecting the decline in their underlying asset values due to the initial offering expenses.

Unfortunately, managers of these closed-end funds, in an effort to keep the price of the shares up, have a history of paying dividends in excess of what their underlying bonds are earning. In effect, they are sending us back our own money as dividends. This obviously cannot go on forever. The history of many of these closed-end funds has been that the dividends are ultimately reduced in order to bring them in line with reality. When the dividend is reduced, that wonderful new closed-end fund share for which we paid $10, now sells for $7.50. Don't ever buy a new, closed-end bond fund! Buy an old one that has already diminished in value if your analysis says that its underlying assets are really worth the lower price.

Bonds For People Who Don't Like Taxes

Nobody likes to pay taxes. Some will do anything to minimize their tax bill and will never buy a bond that is not tax-free. It is not difficult to calculate whether tax-free income makes sense for you. Just look at your top income tax rate and determine whether paying taxes on taxable bond interest or buying a tax-free bond leaves you with the most after-tax cash.

The municipal bond market, where bonds of cities and states are traded, is a large and relatively unregulated market made up of many securities dealers and banks. Over the years, investors have suffered substantial abuse at the hands of municipal bond dealers, including banks, who sell them bonds at outrageous prices or buy bonds from them at well below the market value. Most people have no way to determine the fair market value of municipal bonds. Municipal bond prices are rarely quoted in the newspapers. While any investment counselor will tell you that when buying or selling municipal bonds you should talk to several dealers and get competitive quotes, I have yet to run across very many investors who really do that. It is very important!

Obviously, the bond market is a huge and complex place. We have only scratched the surface and will make no attempt to explore the vast world of foreign bonds, mortgage-backed securities and exotic derivatives traded 24 hours-a-day, 365 days-a-year, across the face of the globe.

I Need Help!

"Gee," I'll bet you are thinking, "Stocks are complicated and difficult to pick. And there seems to be more to this bond buying than I ever imagined. I need help. I'll go to a broker. He'll know what to do!" Beware.

CHAPTER FIVE

THE TRUTH ABOUT STOCKBROKERS

---

*When you are skinning your customers, you should leave
some skin on to grow so that you can skin them again.*
                              — Nikita Khruschev

Before you go running off to stockbrokers looking for trustworthy investment advice, it is important that you understand the brokers' role and the all-pervasive sales culture of the business in which they work.

Stock and bond brokerage is only one part of the larger industry called investment banking. Investment bankers have been around since the Middle Ages when they raised money for warring kings who needed to pay their armies. Early in our country's history they raised the money to build our canals and toll roads. Later they helped the "robber barons" finance our railroads and steel mills. Today the main role of an investment banker is to raise money by selling new stock and bond issues for companies or, perhaps, bonds for school districts that need to build new schools, or cities and states financing hospitals or sewer systems or roads. The major investment banking houses include firms such as Merrill Lynch, Smith Barney, Morgan Stanley, Goldman Sachs, and Salomon Brothers. There are dozens of regional firms like A.G. Edwards, J.C. Bradford, Rauscher Pierce, Raymond James, and Morgan Keegan.

The Investment Banking Business

Investment banking can be an enormously profitable business. One of the largest investment bankers in the United States, Goldman Sachs, earned about $2.5 billion, before partners' compensation and taxes in 1993, ranking it right up there with the biggest companies in the world. At their upper levels, investment banking firms employ very bright people. Most are extraordinarily well-educated, hold advanced degrees, are energetic, creative, highly competitive, and work very hard. They are handsomely paid. Compensation over one million dollars per year is not uncommon on Wall Street.

Competition for both private and public sector investment banking clients is fierce. Most public sector financing is awarded by state and local governments through a competitive bidding process. Companies, however, are wooed. A major company represents a potential long-term fountain of riches for its investment banker. The relationships between companies and their investment bankers often last for many years. A growing company may use its investment banker for decades to manage its stock and bond offerings. The company may also acquire other companies, generating big fees for the investment banker's merger and acquisition specialists.

How Do Investment Bankers Woo Clients?

Every day, investment bankers make sales calls on high-level corporate executives throughout the world. Each solicits business from major companies in its own way but the sales presentations all have similar themes. I think you would benefit from knowing what goes on behind the scenes.

Join The Glitterati

Pretend for a moment that you are the chief executive officer of a large Midwestern manufacturing company being visited by a senior partner of an important New York-based investment banking firm. The sales call will begin with a discussion of the investment banker's current clients. Pointing with pride to a long list of well-known companies, the investment banker will drop the names of their top executives, the glitterati of American business. Indicating an easy familiarity with their comings and goings, any investment banker will subtly attribute much of his clients' business success to his own invaluable assistance. Implicit in all of this is the suggestion that you too could be as successful and rub shoulders with, maybe even play golf with, this distinguished and successful group of executives, if only you were the banker's client.

We Can Sell Anything

The second topic will usually be the strength of the investment banker's distribution capability. Distribution means sales force power. Distribution power is important because it represents the investment banker's ability to get new stock issues sold or new bond issues placed with investors like you and me through their stockbrokers. You will be told of the remarkable ability of the banker's hundreds or thousands of retail stockbrokers to sell any investment product. You will hear about the ability of the firm to syndicate its offerings of stocks and bonds through other investment banking firms who also have enormous sales forces. You will also be told about the investment banker's small but powerful platoon of what are known as "institutional sales people." Smarter and better educated than the retail stockbrokers, they sell to sophisticated buyers such as insurance companies and mutual fund companies that have the ability to buy securities in very large quantities.

The selling power of an investment banking firm is important to corporate managements. Superior distribution capability means their companies' stock and bond issues can be easily sold at high prices and will be parcelled out in small and medium-sized blocks among multitudes of individual and institutional buyers. That, they hope, will protect the companies' securities prices from being unduly depressed by a few big investors who may elect to sell their holdings in the companies' stocks or bonds. Widespread distribution of a company's securities also protects its executives from challenges to their power by large investors who might accumulate threatening amounts of voting power through their large stock holdings. Stockholders get to vote for such things as the election of the companies' directors. Directors have the power to hire and fire the companies' operating executives. Executives are fond of friendly directors and quiescent stockholders.

The other important resource brought to the table by the investment banker is his stock research department. He will note that his firm's research department is staffed by some of Wall Street's most respected analysts, widely followed by important institutional investors. More about research later.

Closing The Sale

Before the investment banker leaves your office, you will probably be invited to lunch on your next trip to New York. If you accept the invitation, you will find yourself in his firm's exquisitely paneled private dining room at its Wall Street headquarters surrounded by gleaming silver, polished crystal, and fine cigars. Often these lunches are hosted by luminaries such as ex-Secretaries of the Treasury, past members of The Federal Reserve Board or other high-profile officials of previous government administrations. They may or may not know

" AND OVER HERE WE HAVE THE FORMER SECRETARIES OF THE TREASURY, DEFENSE, AND COMMERCE, AND, OF COURSE, BART, FROM 'THE YOUNG AND THE RESTLESS'. "

much about business. They are hired by the investment banking firms at very high salaries to impress you with their access to the international halls of power. You can almost smell the prestige. All of this is cloaked in the high integrity and moral traditions of the founders whose portraits adorn the walls. You too can join the glitterati! It all hinges on your company becoming a client of the firm.

over w/ a cloak (loose garment)

Brokerage Firm Research — Be Skeptical

The subject of Wall Street research deserves further explanation. The research departments of Wall Street firms generate those reports you see in brokerage offices that analyze companies and discuss the prospects for their stock. Research coverage of their companies is important to top executives. Almost every top corporate executive believes that if the virtues of his company were better displayed to the investment community, his stock would sell for a higher price. Remember, top executives often hold lots of stock and stock options in the companies they run and they like high stock prices. Like the classic troubled teen who complains that his parents just don't understand him, most of these top executives feel that investors just don't understand their companies, or they would value them higher.

Analysts May Support Clients No Matter What

If you want to see a large company president get really upset just let a major brokerage house come out with a research report saying that his company is a "dog" and that the stock should be sold. That is why you will rarely, if ever, see that kind of comment. Irritated company presidents don't make good sales prospects for investment bankers whose research departments write negative reports. You have probably noticed in looking at opinions on stocks that you see a lot of "hold" recommendations. "Hold" usually means "we think you should sell this but we don't dare say so because this is a big client".

Recently while traveling I came across a classic example of this "support our client" bias too often found in brokerage house research. I was in a city which has one significant investment banking firm. It is a good-size, regional firm with a number of branch brokerage offices. The firm's research director was one of a number of local people, including some stockbrokers, asked by a magazine to name his favorite five stocks, those he believed would be the five best-performing stocks in the world, for entry in a year-long stock picking contest.

Four out of five stocks that he named were his firm's investment banking clients. Can you imagine the coincidence?

It's Not Easy Being An Analyst

Analysts don't have an easy time confronting powerful people who do not like having negative reports written about their firms. You may remember the story of the Philadelphia securities analyst who after working at Janney Montgomery Scott, a Philadelphia investment banking firm for sixteen years, publicly questioned the viability of Donald Trump's 1,250 room Taj Mahal casino. Mr. Roffman, the analyst, said that he expected the Atlantic City, New Jersey casino to be unable to pay the interest on its bonds.

As *The Wall Street Journal* reported, "In casting doubt on the Taj's chances for success, Mr. Roffman encountered a problem familiar to many analysts. The bearer of negative predictions is often criticized by the target company and sometimes by the analyst's own firm."

The day the report was issued, Donald Trump fired off a letter to the president of Janney Montgomery Scott in which he called Mr. Roffman's statements, "An outrage!" He also wrote, "I am now planning to institute a major lawsuit against your firm unless Mr. Roffman makes a major public apology". Rothman was fired. The Taj, of course, couldn't pay the interest on its bonds!

Analysts From The Company Viewpoint

Companies want their stories told favorably and work very hard to maintain good relationships with research analysts from their own investment banking firms as well as those working for other firms. In our businesses, we often entertained research analysts, spending a lot of time explaining our company to them and answering their questions.

In the late 1970s I was the chief financial officer of The Flintkote Company, a large publicly held building materials company. I was often called upon to brief analysts. Normally, analysts would spend a few hours at the company and then write a report much like others previously written about our company by other analysts. I assume they read each other's reports.

Occasionally, we would be visited by analysts who seemed to be real stars. They were the ones who really dug into the facts and tried to understand our company from top to bottom. Two of the best were Michael Steinberg, who worked for an obscure Wall Street firm, and Oscar Schafer who managed money for a very wealthy family group. Some years later, Mike started his own investment management firm which has since prospered. I am sure it has benefitted from his meticulous research. Oscar is now one of the respected investment gurus featured annually in *Barron's* Roundtable.

Cultivating Analysts — The Wal-Mart Model

There is nothing wrong with a company cultivating and educating security analysts. Wal-Mart, one of the greatest corporate success stories of our generation, used to invite bankers and securities analysts from all over the U.S. to Bentonville, Arkansas. They were invited to spend long weekends learning about the company at the time of Wal-Mart's annual shareholders' meeting. Wal-Mart would assign store managers to pick them up at the airport and be their drivers for the weekend. Bankers and analysts would be lavishly entertained, taken on river float trips and exposed in every positive way possible to Wal-Mart, its management, and its operating philosophy. Displaying the remotely located Wal-Mart business to analysts who ultimately wrote glowing reports about the company had a great deal to do with Wal-Mart's success. Without those reports investors would never have heard of Wal-Mart. Once they learned about the company, they were willing to buy Wal-Mart's stock and bonds. The investor relations campaign succeeded in giving Wal-Mart access to the capital markets where the company's ability to raise money was critical to its phenomenal growth.

Research On Non-Clients Can Move Markets

No investment banker can underwrite enough new stock and bond offerings to keep its sales force busy all the time. The research department must continually produce reports in order to give the stockbrokers new ideas that they can pass along to their customers, thereby creating stock trades and earning commissions.

Research reports on companies are issued every day. Some research analysts have developed followings among large institutions. Their opinions can have a significant effect on the stock prices of single companies, or sometimes on the stocks of all the companies in a given industry. Respected analysts can put out a piece of research that gives their firm's sales people the ammunition to create a lot of stock trades. Such trades generate commissions. Commissions are the life blood of the sales force. Some analysts are actually measured and compensated based upon the trading volume and commissions their research generates. You will occasionally hear that "a stock dropped 10 percent today after analysts at Callum & Robbum downgraded their outlook for the company's stock from buy to hold." You can be sure when you hear such financial news that Callum & Robbum's analysts generated some commissions for the firm as they convinced their clients to sell the stock.

Important pieces of research, the kind that moves stock prices up or down, don't usually get delivered to small investors like you and me with the same sense of urgency that they are delivered to large institutional investors. It only makes sense that this "hot" research report will get to the big institution, potentially a buyer or seller of thousands and thousands of shares, long before it reaches the stockbroker in Cincinnati or Laramie, Wyoming, who might be able to use the report to sell a few hundred shares to people like you and me. By the time you pick up a piece of research in your stockbroker's office, you can be sure that it is stale and has been fully acted upon by the marketplace.

Listen To Independent Analysts

Not all analysts work for investment banking firms, some work for research firms that sell their reports to large institutional clients. As a small investor you will probably never see that type of research as it is expensive and has a limited circulation. Other analysts write for independent research organizations such as Value Line or Standard & Poor's. That information is readily available to you at the public library. It is an excellent source for gathering historical data on companies. It is not usually timely enough to affect the markets. Analysts not directly connected with investment banking firms can escape the bias that so often is apparent in brokerage house research. They are free to "tell it like it is", good or bad.

How Good Is Stock Research Anyway?

Don't underestimate the difficulty that a research analyst has in trying to predict the financial performance of a complicated business a year or two in the future. Any seasoned executive, who has participated in the planning and budgeting process for a large business, will tell you that, try as they might to be exact, it is an uncertain effort. Great attention is paid to sales forecasts, expense forecasts, production plans, and staffing. Division by division, the numbers are put together with meticulous detail. All of these numbers, when finally brought together, become the basis for the overall company budget. The year wears on, unforeseen events intervene, and the company's final results may bear little resemblance to that meticulously prepared budget.

Securities analysts are not included in the budget process so their jobs are much more complicated. Not only are they not privy to the facts, they are many steps removed from the action. If the top executives can't accurately forecast the final numbers a year or two in advance, how can they be expected to do any better? Interestingly enough, I never met a company chairman who would even attempt to forecast his company's stock price a year or two in advance, certainly not in public. Analysts attempt it every day.

New Stock Issues — How They Are Priced

As a potential investor, it is important to understand how new issues of stocks are priced. Here we are speaking of new stock issues for companies "going public" for the first time. Don't confuse this with the new closed-end fund issues that I advised you to avoid.

Anyone who has ever had to deal with top corporate executives of large companies knows that they can be very tough negotiators. They are usually nice people but you can bet they are going to be strong advocates for their companies' positions. An investment banker, who is working with the top executives of a company to price a new stock issue, is caught between the demanding executives of the company who want the stock sold at the highest possible price, and the marketplace. The investment banker knows that if the issue is so overpriced that its value plummets once it is sold by those squads of retail sales people, he may have done a lot of damage to his distribution division. Those legions of sales people can't afford to infuriate scores of customers. A little loss is one thing, a big loss is something else entirely. A cardinal rule is that you don't "blow up" clients by causing them big losses!

Investment bankers are not in the business of protecting buyers. They will try to get us to pay as much for a new share of stock as possible without risking "blowing us up". Before a new stock issue comes to market, as part of their selling effort, the investment bankers will usually travel around the country with some of the company's top executives. Their purpose is to explain the company and its new stock issue to large, potential buyers. These meetings, called "road shows" in the trade, often cover subjects not written into the prospectus. They are not supposed to, but they do. Companies are not allowed to make earnings projections in their prospectuses. But in an informal setting like a road show the company executives may give indications of what they expect the company to earn in the next year or two. As a small investor you are not privy to these discussions of information that may be critically important to you.

Typically, a new stock issue will be priced so that the initial purchasers will have a small profit when the shares begin to trade in the market. If the new issue rises 10 to 15 percent, the buyers will be happy and most will hold onto the stock. The investment bankers will have made a successful trade-off between the demands of their client, the company, and their own stockbrokers who need to keep customers happy.

Now you know why it is usually impossible to get a meaningful number of shares in an attractive new stock issue from your broker. If he or she is going to give anybody an automatic profit by allocating a significant number of shares to them, he or she is going to be sure that they are very important customers, not penny ante players like you and me. Beware of buying new issues that are not hard to get! It is a clear signal that the broker is having a hard time placing the shares.

Usually about four to six weeks after a new issue is sold to the public, the brokerage firm who sold the new issue will publish a follow-up research report on the company. The purpose of the report is to give the stock price a little boost and continuing support in after-market trading. The report also makes management of the company that is issuing the stock happy.

Research into the behavior of new stock issues indicates that buying them after the initial public offering, when they have already traded up in price, is frequently not a profitable strategy. Investor enthusiasm for the stocks cools, research coverage becomes more infrequent, and they languish.

"We Are All Big Boys" — The Culture

The overriding and disturbing phrase that you hear time and time again at the highest levels of Wall Street is, "We are all big boys." It is pervasive throughout the business and means, "Buyer, beware!" Unfortunately, we are not all sophisticated big boys; we are senior citizens, widows never before faced with investing money, and busy people working hard to put children through school and save for retirement. Few people without an extensive accounting and legal background can read and understand the prospectus which accompanies a new stock offering, even though they are expected to rely on it for all of their information.

My wife's father, a cotton man, died when he was only 43. The cotton business had been lousy for the previous few years and the family was left in rather dire financial straits. My mother-in-law had some savings and sought the investment advice of a family friend, a local stockbroker. The family friend invested her total savings in some highly speculative municipal bonds which were dependent for their ability to pay interest on a developmental stage gas utility distribution system in a rural area of east Tennessee. Needless to say, the gas development failed and the bonds defaulted. When she asked the family friend why he had put her in such a speculative investment, he answered, "That is what you told me you wanted". I guess he thought she was a "big boy." It is interesting to note, the bonds were sold with the highest commission imaginable, somewhere around 10 percent.

Intimidation And Sales Pressure

Brokers can be quite intimidating in their sales efforts. A couple of years ago, one of our clients asked that we accept the management of her mother's sizeable account. Mrs. Castle, a quiet and gentle lady, had been dealing with an aggressive young broker from a major national firm. The young broker inherited the sales responsibility for Mrs. Castle's account after her late husband's broker of many years retired. The young broker continually put Mrs. Castle under intense pressure to sell long-held investments suggesting that she re-invest the money in the broker's in-house financial products. If Mrs. Castle attempted to resist she was literally brow beaten until she went along. Fortunately, her children stepped in and took control of the situation.

In a similar case, an aggressive broker who had been selling bonds to an older lady in failing health moved from one brokerage firm to another. Prior to leaving the first firm, the broker sold all the client's bonds and high commission mutual funds, buying virtually the same ones back at the new firm soon after arriving. If one commission is good, two must be better!

Television brokerage advertising presents exactly the opposite view of the industry's "we are all big boys" cultural bias. In warm and fuzzy TV ads, helpful brokers have listened to their clients in years past and made it possible for the widow to stay comfortably in her home after her husband passes away. A wise and bespeckled gentleman assures you with great sincerity that his firm takes care of one customer at a time.

Brokers Disguised As Bankers

People who are skeptical of brokers and who would never listen to a sales person can be easily fooled when they buy investment products from a bank. Banks, hungry for revenue and unable to retain depositors' money in low-interest CDs, are now selling investment products from desks in their lobbies.

Alice's husband worked at Sears for his entire business career. Under Sears' stock purchase plan he had retired with a substantial holding. Some years later he died leaving Alice the Sears' stock. Alice understood the "too many eggs in one basket" problem and decided to do something about it. Alone, cautious, and wary of brokers, Alice went to a local bank that she trusted. She had worked for them many years ago and expected them to act in her best interest. Alice asked them to help her sell some of the Sears stock so that she could diversify her holdings. The helpful banker sold her Sears stock, and then talked her into buying a very high commission annuity, an insurance product. Alice had no need for the annuity. She is now trapped in the wrong investment by a very high redemption penalty of about eight percent, or $8,000 on a $100,000 investment. Alice can't bring herself to sell the annuity and take the loss. What she didn't understand was that this "broker in disguise" was taking advantage of her.

Investor's Business Daily reported in April, 1994 that thousands of banks were using mutual fund companies and brokers to help sell investments to consumers unhappy with low bank interest rates. From their standpoint fund companies and brokers have come to view banks as sales channels with huge potential. Frequently, branch bank managers don't have direct control over the sales people working in their lobbies. These representatives work for marketing companies hired by the banks. The article further noted, "Some bank branches now have sales people making more than $200,000, working along-side branch managers making $40,000, and parking lots where tellers' Ford Escorts jostle for space with sales people's BMW 750s."

There is enormous abuse of naive consumers by sales representatives in bankers' garb. The financial service companies that create annuities, mutual funds, and other financial products know that these bank lobby sales representatives can be enormously effective at pushing their products. The sales representatives are being given incentives, ranging from trinkets to 40-inch color television sets and trips to Hawaii, to push certain investments. Guidelines within the banking industry specify that compensation should not influence financial product sales, but clearly it does.

Watch Out For Annuities

Tax-deferred annuities like the one Alice bought at the bank appear at first glance to be a very attractive investment for people in high-income tax brackets. They are treated by the Internal Revenue Service as insurance products even though the insurance provisions are usually minimal. Qualifying them as insurance policies allows the build-up of cash values from either interest or investment gains within the annuity to accumulate on a tax-deferred basis. The annuity gives the owner a number of years for compound interest to work without interference from the tax collector. Usually the annuity offers a number of stock and bond options. The owner can choose to have his money invested in one or more of these pools. Taxes only have to be paid when money is periodically taken out of the annuity sometime in the future. Tax-deferred annuities seem ideal for building retirement programs.

Unfortunately, the primary benefit of the annuity — keeping the tax collector at bay while the investment funds within the annuity compound — is usually offset by the disadvantages of the annuity contract. Annuities offer very high sales commissions to the sales people who sell them. The high surrender penalties that are assessed against an owner who decides to take money out of an annuity in the early years of its life are used to cover those high sales commissions. Even if the annuity is not surrendered during the high redemption penalty period, most annuities have very high internal costs. These costs reduce the annual investment returns generated by the stock and bond investments. In addition, annuities are issued under very complex contracts. The contract provisions result in the inflexibilities that most of us would expect from anything having to do with insurance companies.

By the mid-1990s, a few companies were offering annuities designed to overcome most of these disadvantages. Vanguard, Charles Schwab & Co., and Fidelity Investments had entered the field and were beginning to offer very low-cost annuities with more attractive internal investment options. Not found for sale in bank lobbies or by insurance sales persons, they are worthy of further exploration.

Bad Investments - Not Always The Brokers' Fault

Putting people into bad investments is not always the stockbrokers' fault. Sometimes the investing public will just not invest in the things that are the best for them. Clearly, the period following the

October 1987 stock market crash was a wonderful time to buy stocks. No broker could make a living selling stocks at that time because frightened investors wouldn't listen and wouldn't buy.

After the stock market crash in October 1987, investors were very safety-conscious. The only thing they would buy were products such as "guaranteed", closed-end government bond funds. The brokers, ever ready to meet the demand, rushed to put together these funds and some 44 new issues were launched over the ensuing months. Of the 44 issues, 38 fell an average of 17.5 percent in value in the first four months they were publicly traded. Your local broker may not have been astute enough to know that these were terrible investments. I cannot help but believe that his superiors knew what bad products they were foisting off on a frightened public.

In May 1988, *The Wall Street Journal* reported that the Securities and Exchange Commission was studying this closed-end fund "mystery." The paper further reported that, "John W. Peavy, III, chairman of the finance department at Southern Methodist University in Dallas, who has done research on closed-end fund issues, says he wonders why any investor would buy a new closed-end issue. Such investing, he says, is seemingly irrational activity."

Brokers - Unscrupulous or Uneducated?

The stockbrokerage business is a tough business. In my opinion, it is not really any more populated by the unscrupulous than any other sales driven industry. The danger is that many stockbrokers, far from the action and viewed with disdain by the insiders in Wall Street, are viewed erroneously by their clients as experts. Any bright high school graduate can be taught enough to get his license to sell stocks in about six months. Many are actually incompetent when it comes to investing money.

The manager of a large brokerage office once described for me the "ideal" candidate for their brokerage training program. "About 30-years-old, they will have had some past sales experience calling on upper-income customers. A pharmaceutical salesperson who had been calling on doctors is perfect. They shouldn't be too smart, otherwise, they won't follow instructions and sell their customers what we tell them to sell."

I was sitting in my office one day in 1991 when my partner walked in with a friend of his, a successful stockbroker who works for one of the large national brokerage firms. His friend Jack Billings was in a state of high agitation. He warned me that we should immediately liquidate all of our stock fund investments because the price/earnings ratio of the Dow Jones Industrial Average was at a very high level. That would indicate an overpriced stock market. A little analysis would have shown him that if you eliminated the results of the two or three very large money-losing firms that were represented in the thirty stock average, you would come up with a much more reasonable result. The market wasn't overpriced. I wonder how many investors he scared out of the market?

We work for a number of corporate clients who have profit-sharing retirement plans for their employees. These clients usually hire actuarial consulting firms to handle the specialized accounting and tax issues involved with their plans. Actuarial consultants see hundreds of plans and annually report back to their clients on their investment results. One of the largest actuarial consultants that we know has told us that he has never seen a plan, managed by a retail stockbroker, that has ever made money consistently.

Brokers Disguised As Consultants

If you serve in the role of trustee of a retirement plan or are on the board of an endowed institution or have oversight responsibility for a large amount of pension or endowment money, beware the broker disguised as an impartial investment consultant. Following the enactment of the Employment Retirement Income Security Act of 1974 (ERISA), people with oversight responsibility for the operation of pension and profit-sharing plans became very concerned about the potential liability they might have for the investment results of those plans. Theoretically, they could be sued by any plan participant for almost any mistake.

Fanning the flames of this fear, which has not turned out to be well founded, a number of firms were established by brokers to be "independent and objective" consultants to trustees and fiduciaries. They often claim to share the trustees' responsibility for the prudent investment of the retirement money. These quasi-independents produce elaborate charts and graphs tracking investment results. They also screen professional money management firms, purporting to recommend those that are most likely to do a good job managing the money for the trustees. Many suggest to you as a trustee that their services are essentially free. The consultants' services will be paid for at no cost to the pension plan. They explain that if some of the commissions generated from securities trades, which will take place in any event, are directed through their brokerage affiliate, they will use those commissions to offset their consulting fees. About 95 percent of the firms in the pension consulting business operate that way. Don't use one!

The pension consulting business is rife with abuses. As brokers in disguise, these firms depend on commissions flowing through their brokerage affiliates for their livelihood. Frequently if you ask them to do a "search" for a qualified money management firm, you will be steered toward a firm that is already giving them commission business.

The industry is a "pay-to-play" industry. Investment managers who "pay up" get recommended. When you are shown their results, they are often measured against conveniently contrived universes of other managers whose investment results they appear to outdo. Stick with reputable consultants who do not have brokerage affiliates and who, like lawyers and CPAs, are directly compensated for their time.

The Most Dangerous Broker Of All

Aside from "penny stock" brokers who are akin to armed muggers and other felons, the most dangerous firms with which individuals could do business are the small municipal bond firms. In the Mid-South, there is a large bank that for many years has had an active sales force selling bonds to small country banks and individuals. At one time, many country bankers fancied themselves bond experts, making them easy to fleece as they bought bonds for their little rural banks. The bond-selling business has proven extraordinarily lucrative for the large city bank. The career path to the president's office has often been through the bond department.

Years ago, a few of the bank's better bond sales people, realizing how much money there was to be made in the business, quit the bank and started their own bond businesses. Out of that genesis in the late-1950s and early-1960s has grown an enormous number of high-pressure bond sales operations spreading throughout the country.

Tales of bond sales practices are legendary Operated out of large rooms filled with desks and telephones, manned by sales people with about two weeks of training, the firms are beehives of activity. Their business practices include pinning one-hundred-dollar bills to the wall to be taken down by the next sales person making a sale over the telephone, providing big producers with leased luxury cars if they are top sales persons of the month, passing out Rolex watches, and paying big commissions. One notorious pioneer used to pass out Benzedrine pills to his sales people to keep them "pumped up" for making "cold" telephone calls to unsuspecting victims.

The macho culture of the bond business is not confined to small "boiler rooms" in the financial backwaters. *Liars' Poker*, a hilarious, but bitingly critical book written by Michael Lewis, detailed equally predatory trading practices at one of the largest bond trading houses in the world, Salomon Brothers.

In the early 1980s, my wife and I lived in south Florida and attended a seminar in Boca Raton. The advertising for the seminar was intriguing because it promised 12 percent tax-free returns on municipal bonds. We went to see what kind of product the brokers were selling to the large number of affluent retirees who lived in our area. The seminar, incidentally, offered a free lunch. The lunch, tailored to the age of the average attendee, turned out to be a soft chicken salad sandwich.

The product being pushed by the handsome young man with the appealing smile and polished presentation turned out to be tax-free bonds sold to finance nursing homes. They were being sold by a notorious group of bad actors operating out of Jackson, Mississippi. Knowing something about the business, I was probably the only person in the room who knew that a couple of the bond issues the young man discussed so glowingly were already in default on their interest payments.

There Are Some Good Brokers

Many bright young people enter the brokerage business with a sincere interest in helping their clients. They have a very difficult time with the ethical conflicts implicit in "making quota" as the firms demand, and they usually leave. If you have a good broker, appreciate your luck.

What Now?

If picking stocks is hard, and bonds are complicated and not nearly as safe as you thought, and you need to be skeptical of stockbrokers, where are you to turn? Take a lesson from how very large companies or cities and states invest their employee pension money.

CHAPTER SIX

INVESTING AS THE PROFESSIONALS DO

Hitch your wagon to a star.   — *Ralph Waldo Emerson*

If you were a big investor — either a very wealthy individual with tens of millions of dollars, or a person in charge of overseeing a large pension fund such as that of the state of California which has many billions of dollars worth of assets — you would not attempt to manage the portfolio yourself. Like most other big investors, you would not deal with stockbrokers but instead would hire a number of money management firms to handle your portfolio. Money management firms vary in size — from very large organizations with lots of talented experts managing billions of dollars for hundreds of clients, all the way down to small firms with perhaps a few professionals managing more modest amounts of money for a smaller number of clients.

Can I Hire A Money Management Firm?

As a practical matter you and I run into problems when considering hiring money management firms for ourselves. They are almost
always organized to work for very large investors. Many will not take
money under supervision unless the account is at least $1,000,000.
There are some money managers who have minimums as high as
$50,000,000. Clearly, these managers are only interested in working
for big institutional clients such as large companies or governmental
entities. But as small investors, we can still learn a lot of valuable
lessons from how these large institutions do their investing. Let's look
into it more closely.

What Exactly Is A Money Management Firm?

Some money management firms are large enough to manage a
full spectrum of U.S. stocks, foreign stocks, bonds and other more
exotic types of securities. Most, however, are specialists, concentrat-
ing on a more narrow part of the stock or bond markets and usually
operating with a well-defined philosophy. They may, for instance,
specialize in small, fast-growing technology stocks, or perhaps, just
in stocks of financial companies such as banks, thrifts, and insurance
companies. They may call themselves "growth" investors looking for
fast-growing companies in which to invest, or "value" investors comb-
ing the securities markets for stocks they think are currently undervalued, but that are likely to be discovered soon and then run up in
price.

The people who make the major investment decisions for these
firms are usually seasoned investors. Most began their careers in research departments of brokerage houses, or in the investment departments of insurance companies, or even in bank trust departments.
The real stars in those areas eventually reach salary limitations, and
many move on to money management firms where they can earn
more money. Some may start their own firms. Many who gravitate

toward money management firms do so to escape the inherent ethical conflicts in the brokerage business which pits the interest of brokerage firms and their clients against each other. You remember the "we are all big boys" cultural ethic described in Chapter Five. As independent money managers, these professionals escape the ethical conflict and have the freedom to devote themselves single-mindedly to producing the best returns possible for their clients.

As smaller investors, we don't have access to these experts in the same way larger investors do. Even if we could meet the very large account minimum requirements of one of these money management firms, we would be unwise to place all of our money with one manager, who usually has only one specialty and one style of selecting investments. The big investors, such as large pension plans, hire a number of different managers with different styles and specialties. They divide their portfolios into pieces, giving different pieces to different managers. This diversification is all important and it applies to managers just like it does to individual stocks. The big investor is spreading his risk so that no one money manager who has a bad year can spoil the total portfolio return. It is the same idea as you and I buying a lot of different stocks instead of just a few. The stock that performs terribly can't have a significant impact on our total portfolio.

"Well," you might say, "This all sounds great and I am glad that you've told me about it, but I don't have enough money to hire one money manager, much less multiple money managers."

Where Are The Best Investment Managers?

There is a way for you to benefit from the expertise of these money managers. Prior to 1988 I had firmly believed that buying diversified stock and bond portfolios was the best way to manage money for our clients. However, after reading an article in the June 1988 *Forbes* magazine, I began to re-think that strategy.

The article analyzed the investment returns of the best of the large money management firms for the five years ending in March of that year. Ten managers, all of whom had been in business for a number of years, were profiled. Each managed a substantial amount of money — the smallest $276,000,000, the largest $3.5 billion. Their average annual return over the five-year period was 21.2 percent. These outstanding managers could afford to be picky about taking on new business. *Forbes* reported that most would not take accounts under $1,000,000 and some weren't accepting new money at all.

I thought to myself at the time that if there were only some way to allocate some of our clients' money to this kind of money manager, in fact hiring several different ones for each portfolio, it would be a great way to diversify and get excellent returns. But there didn't seem to be an answer to the size problem, our client accounts were just too small.

Then we discovered the solution — a way for smaller investors to get the benefits of using the world's best money managers. The answer we found was in no-load mutual funds. We analyzed the best of no-load mutual funds shortly after reading the *Forbes* article, and found surprising results. Using the same criteria that *Forbes* had used in rating the money managers, we examined and rated no-load mutual funds. We found that many of the same money managers who had performed well enough to score in the top ten of the *Forbes* analysis also managed some of the top-ranked no-load mutual funds in our analysis.

In fact, the top manager in the *Forbes* study also managed no-load mutual funds. So did four other of the *Forbes* top ten. Eureka! We could retain some of the best money managers in the country and end run their high account minimums by simply buying into the no-load mutual funds that they ran with the same effort, judgment, and brain power that they applied to their big institutional accounts.

Why Do Star Managers Run Mutual Funds?

You may wonder why any of these star money managers, involved with huge amounts of investment dollars for very large investors, would bother to manage a publicly available mutual fund. There are two answers. First, it can be very profitable. A mutual fund company that charges one percent to manage a $1 billion fund earns about $10 million in annual revenue. You can imagine how much money they can make managing a $5 billion or $10 billion fund, much less something as big as Fidelity's Magellan Fund, which in 1994 had over $34.2 billion in assets.

The second reason is that a mutual fund is a highly visible investment. A manager who manages a mutual fund has his results chronicled for all to see on a daily, weekly, monthly, quarterly and annual basis. The results will be measured against all other funds of the same type. If the fund does extremely well, the manager can point with pride to his results. His firm will get great publicity. Publicity is invaluable when his firm competes for business. In attempting to get a contract to manage a portion of a large employee pension fund, like that maintained by the telephone company or General Motors, the sale is much easier with a publicly documented track record of the manager's performance. This is a powerful selling tool. As you can imagine, money management firms that run mutual funds pay a lot of attention to them.

So Where Do Money Managers Invest Their Money?

You might think that Wall Street professionals who have access to private investment pools for the wealthy, many of whom only accept accounts of $5,000,000 or more instead of our usual $2,000 IRA contribution, would choose to invest their money with managers that are not accessible to you and me. Surprisingly, in a March 11, 1994 article, *USA TODAY* reported that William Kapner, managing partner of New York-based Investment Data, polled 135 Wall Street professionals to see who they would choose to manage their own money. Seventy-one percent named a mutual fund manager as the professional they would most like to manage their money other than themselves. The top vote-getter was Ralph Wanger, manager of the two-billion-dollar Acorn Fund, and the 1.5-billion-dollar Acorn International Fund.

What Is A Mutual Fund?

Before we go any further, let me address what might be an obvious question for you: "What is a mutual fund?"

A mutual fund can be thought of as a big pot full of cash and securities held somewhere by a trustee, usually a large bank that safeguards the cash and securities for shareholders. Each shareholder in the fund owns a small interest in the total pool of assets. The assets are not managed by the trustee, but by a money manager, someone who is hired to make buy and sell decisions for this big pool of assets.

You will find that every mutual fund's objective is clearly spelled out in the descriptive information contained in the fund's prospectus. There can be all sorts of different objectives from attempting to maximize growth of capital to maximizing current income. It is the manager's job to accomplish those objectives for us as fund shareholders. Managers are compensated by small percentage fees paid out of the funds. It is in their best interest to do a good job for us. If they do such a good job that the fund grows, both from investment results and from attracting new money from investors, their fees will grow as well. They are very clearly on our side.

Basic Types Of Mutual Funds:

Open-End Funds

Mutual funds are two basic types. "Open-end" funds are those in which we can buy shares, say for $10, and our $10 gets invested in the asset pool at net asset value. Net asset value is determined by valuing everything in the pool the day we buy our shares, on a per share basis. Suppose the stocks and bonds in the asset pool were worth $2,000 and there were 2,000 shares outstanding. Simple arithmetic says that the value of the stocks and bonds underlying each share would be one dollar. If we put $10 in the pool that day, we would be entitled to 10 shares. Our $10 would go into the pool and at the end of the day there would be $2,010 in total value underlying the now outstanding 2,010 shares.

Suppose four or five years later, no new shareholders had purchased shares in the fund, but our smart money manager, with his growth objective firmly in mind, had managed to double the value of the underlying stock and bond assets to $4,020. We could redeem our shares that day for two dollars per share, cashing out at the net asset value per share. A double in five years is pretty good and we would probably feel proud of the good judgment we had used making our investment.

When you see open-end it means that you buy shares at net asset value or redeem shares at net asset value. Most of the funds that we are going to discuss will be open-end funds, they are the most common.

Closed-End Funds

"Closed-end" funds are a little different. You will remember that we touched on closed-end bond funds in our discussion of bonds in Chapter Four and in Chapter Five on brokers. I warned you not to buy a new closed-end bond fund, because they tend to lose value shortly after we buy them. My warning extends to new closed-end funds of any kind.

A closed-end fund has a fixed number of shares. The funds are organized by investment bankers and the money raised through the sale of new shares is pooled together. Closed-end funds are usually dedicated to investing in stocks of companies operating in one industry or perhaps stocks of companies operating in one foreign country. Some, as we have discussed earlier, are formed to invest in bonds. They are usually created and sold when the public's interest in a given area of investing is at a fever pitch. That makes it easy for investment bankers and their stockbrokers to sell the shares. Closed-end funds have been put together to invest solely in stocks of broadcasting and media companies, health care companies and even Turkish industrial companies. As far as I know, the last closed-end fund sold to the public which invested in biotechnology and health care stocks when they were avidly sought by the public came to market at $15 a share in late 1991, right before those stocks swooned. The closed-end fund shares quickly dropped to about $10, resulting in a painful 33 percent loss to the initial investors.

Once the new shares are sold to investors, the pool is closed. There are no sales of shares directly from the fund and no share redemptions by the fund. The fund shares trade freely in the marketplace just like any shares of stock and may trade at above or below the net asset value of the underlying stock or bond assets in the pool.

Seasoned Closed-End Funds May Be Bargains

Once closed-end fund shares have traded in the marketplace for a while, they can often be bought rather cheaply. As investor interest in the particular class of underlying assets dissipates and the selling brokers, having earned their high initial offering commissions, lose interest in the fund shares, they frequently trade down to discounts from their net asset value. If you like the idea of investing in the underlying assets, and can sometimes buy $10 worth of underlying assets at a discount, say at $8.50 per share, you may be able to make a good bit of money. If investors once again get excited about owning the type of underlying assets in the pool, you may get not only the positive effect of their price appreciation but the discount from their net asset value may narrow as well. The shares could even begin to sell at a premium to their underlying asset value, giving you a big gain. Obviously, this is a tricky bet. Things can go against you. Asset values can drop and discounts widen. You have to be right both about the future course of the discount and the price change of the underlying assets to be successful.

Mutual Fund Marketing — Load And No-Load

Mutual funds are run by investment management companies that are, like everybody, in business to make money. Because they charge so little to manage the assets in a mutual fund, usually about one percent per year, they can't make much money unless they can attract a lot of assets into their fund. As we have seen, one percent of a big fund can generate a lot of revenue.

Funds are marketed to investors like you and me in two very different ways, either through brokers who earn commissions for selling them, or directly from the fund management companies with no intervening broker. Mutual funds sold by commission brokers are called "load" funds. Load means commission. No-load means no commission. Some funds are sold both ways, causing great consternation to commissioned brokers who don't like for us to be able to buy them "wholesale". The method of distribution is chosen by the mutual fund company when it determines its marketing plan.

Is There A Performance Difference Between Load And No-Loads?

There is really no difference in the performance or the internal management fees of mutual funds that can be attributed to the way they are sold. There are funds that have good performance, funds that have terrible performance, funds that have high internal costs, and funds that have low internal costs. Some are sold as load funds, some are sold as no-loads. Brokers will tell you, in trying to justify loads, that no-loads have hidden fees and are just as expensive as funds sold with brokerage commissions. Absolutely not true! Usually the brokers are referring to 12b-1 fees, small fees the funds use to pay for advertising. Many funds sold with loads also have 12b-1 charges, so there is no clear distinction. The only reason to ever buy a load fund would be that you were willing to pay to have the broker choose the fund for you. With a little work, you can certainly make these choices at least as effectively for yourself. When you make your own decisions you know there will be no hidden agenda.

This Is The Fund For You!

One of the problems with buying mutual funds from commission brokers is those hidden agendas. Incentives in the brokerage business pay brokers more to sell some funds than others. It has not been uncommon for the large brokerage houses to pay their stock-brokers more for selling their own in-house funds than other, perhaps superior, products. A *Wall Street Journal* article published July 27, 1993, noted that Paine Webber was forced to pay an award to five former brokers who accused the firm of forcing them from their jobs after they balked at selling Paine Webber proprietary products to their clients. The article continued, "The brokers were pressured to place the interest of the house first, the house second, and the house third." Asserted the lawyer for the brokers, "A broker should place his clients first, the house second, and himself third."

Hidden Commissions - Find The Load

Any mutual fund that you buy from a commissioned stockbroker, even if the broker is disguised as a banker, has a commission load attached somewhere. The competition created by the remarkable growth of the no-load fund industry has forced sellers of load funds to go to great lengths to hide the loads. The most common technique is to hide the load in the fine print and charge you a big exit penalty when you sell the fund. That is why you will see the same mutual fund sold through a brokerage firm with A, B, and C shares. The fund is the same, the way you pay the brokerage commission differs. On A shares, you pay a front-end load. On B shares, the load is hidden and there is a declining surrender penalty. The broker gets paid on the front end no matter what. On C shares, which are relatively new, you pay an annual fee of about one percent for as long as you own the fund. To get to the heart of the matter, and find out where the charges are hidden, just ask the broker, "What if I want to get out tomorrow?" He will have to explain it to you.

The Big Problem With Loads

We are not against commissions. Lots of people, such as real estate sales people work for commissions, do a good job and we are happy to pay them. As you will see later, the problem with paying commissions and buying load funds is that from time to time you are going to have to sell one and buy another. To a limited degree you can sometimes do that without a commission load if you switch funds within one "family" of funds. Limiting your options to one family, however, eliminates your ability to venture into many other attractive fund investments. Paying high commissions each time you moved your money from one fund to another more promising one would make it virtually impossible for you to make money.

It is not my intention to make you an expert in the selection and buying and selling of no-load mutual funds. There are lots of good books that have been produced on the subject and the world does not need another. However, I will tell you that one of the best books on the subject is *The Handbook for No-Load Fund Investors* by Sheldon Jacobs. (His phone number and address can be found in Appendix C.) If you are really into detailed research, go to the library and ask for the Morningstar reports or Value Line's Mutual Fund Survey. Both contain exhaustive descriptions of thousands of funds.

A Word About "Wrap" Accounts

By the late 1980s stockbrokers were recognizing that they had lost their credibility as sources of investment advice to a large part of the investing public. They had to do something to try to maintain their market position. The brokers' solution was to go to investors and say, "Look, why don't you let us find a professional investment advisor whose style fits your own special needs. The advisor wouldn't ordinarily be willing to take your account but because we can bring him a lot of business from different clients, he will agree to manage your $100,000 account. As brokers, we will only charge you one fee of three percent of the account value per year to cover all of the trading costs and the money manager's fee." This arrangement is known in the brokerage business as a "wrap fee" arrangement. Wrap accounts are appealing to unsophisticated investors. They have been easy to sell and the wrap fee business has enjoyed phenomenal growth.

There are lots of drawbacks to wrap fee accounts. The first is the level of fees. Three percent annually seems to be a rather common fee. If the long-term rate of return on diversified stock portfolios is around 10 percent, you cannot afford to give up almost one-third of the expected return in fees. Secondly, there is a real concern that money managers who manage wrap fee accounts do not attempt to negotiate the most favorable trading executions for their clients. These factors can add materially to the hidden cost of operating your account and can seriously impact performance. Remember, the wrap money manager has gotten on the brokerage firm's approved list of money managers by being willing to cut his normal management fees, splitting them with the brokers. The wrap manager has also agreed to run all the commissions generated from your account through the broker. His real allegiance is going to be to the brokerage firm who is sending client assets to him, not to you as an individual client. You will probably never see or meet the manager.

More important, when you enter into one of these expensive arrangements, you are effectively putting all of your eggs in one basket. You have chosen one manager with one speciality. No large investor would ever consider doing that.

Buy Good Funds And Put Them Away? . . . Maybe Not

"Well," you have probably concluded, "If I could build my own investment portfolio by picking out some of these no-load mutual funds run by star managers, I could have the best of all possible worlds. Not only would each fund represent a diversified portfolio of stocks or bonds, but I would have also have effectively hired some of the best investment minds in the country to manage the money. On top of all that, like the big guys who run pension funds, I would be diversified among money managers. If one had a bad year, it should not destroy the overall performance of my portfolio. In any event, the manager with the bad year would probably bounce back the next." That's what I used to think. But there is a lot more to it.

CHAPTER SEVEN

WHAT SMALLER INVESTORS NEED TO KNOW ABOUT MONEY MANAGERS

Business more than any other occupation is a continual dealing with the future. It is a continual calculation, an instinctive exercise in foresight.

— *Henry R. Luce*

In working for large companies, I was involved with selecting people to manage portions of our employee pension funds. We would ask our actuarial consulting firm, quite a legitimate one by the way, to pre-screen some money managers who might be appropriate for the assignment. The consultants would usually winnow down the candidates until they had about five or six to present, and from which our committee would make a selection.

All of the candidates who made it through the pre-screening process looked pretty good. They all had good track records, usually five years or more. They had references from their other clients and, when we met with them, each talked intelligently about investing. They discoursed at great length on what methods they would use for choosing investments depending on the role we wanted them to play in the overall management of the portfolio.

We would select a manager, perhaps as much for his or her pleasing personality as anything else. In reality because of careful pre-screening, they were probably all about equal in skill level.

All of us on the committee had plenty of other responsibilities involved with running a large company. If it wasn't manufacturing problems or union negotiations or trying to keep our bankers happy with us, it was something else. We would probably not pay too much attention to the pension plan until we held a quarterly or annual review meeting to look over the results.

Many times the results of either a new manager, or even one that had been around for a while, would prove disappointing. Sure that our selection process had not been flawed, we would usually give the manager another year or two to prove himself. Often, the results did not improve and we would have to go through the unpleasant experience of terminating a manager whom we genuinely enjoyed as a person. You get to know these people, they may occasionally call and take you to lunch. You may even meet their spouses and learn about their children. Like having to fire an employee, it is always difficult and, because we were sympathetic towards the manager, we probably put the decision off longer than we should have.

The Track Record Trap — Changing Styles

It wasn't until some years later, that I realized we were falling into the same trap that individual investors frequently fall into when selecting mutual funds for investment. We were basing our selections almost exclusively on track records rather than trying to figure out what was likely to happen in the future. Money management firms have their own specialties and definite styles of investing. One style can be in favor and will work quite well, if market conditions are right, for a few years. The style can stop working and produce poor results for an equally long time. The fund managers don't suddenly have an IQ attack, the market simply moves away from them and committed to a style of investing, they cannot change.

"Value" Managers — Bargain Buyers

Probably the two most commonly discussed styles of investing are "value" and "growth". We touched on these styles earlier. Value investors produced very good results in the United States stock market from sometime in the early 1980s until about the end of the third quarter of 1989. Value investors try to find companies whose shares are selling much cheaper than what they believe these companies are really worth. A favorite technique is for a value investor to look at a company and ask himself, "What would this company be worth to an intelligent buyer who could buy the whole thing in a fair market transaction?" If the answer seems to be that somebody would pay a whole lot more for the company than the share price reflects, the value investor will buy the stock in the hope that the market will one day recognize the true value of the company and the shares will rise in price.

Value In The 1980s — Takeover Targets

This was a magic approach throughout most of the 1980s. That was a period when one corporation was taking over another in a merger almost every week. Investment bankers who arranged mergers and acquisitions, and corporations on the prowl for business opportunities were constantly looking for undervalued takeover targets. In essence, value managers, merger and acquisition specialists, and corporate managers were using the same selection criteria. Any value manager worth his salt was going to have some of his stock investments in these takeover targets purchased from him at higher prices in corporate mergers, thereby producing good investment returns for his clients, or in our case, shareholders in his mutual fund.

Junk Bonds As Takeover Currency

Corporate acquisitions were very easy to finance with "junk bonds" up until about the end of 1989. Junk bond is the euphemistic title given to any corporate bond issued by a company smaller than about the top 100 companies in the United States. Technically any bond rated below BBB is known in the industry as "junk" (see Appendix A). It doesn't necessarily mean the quality is terrible, but sometimes it does. In about 1989, some of the acquisitions done earlier in the decade began to go sour. Some of the aggressive acquirers were unable to pay interest on the junk bond debt they had used to purchase the target companies. Alarm bells went off in the minds of junk bond buyers and lenders such as the Savings & Loans that had been big sources of funds. Suddenly there was no more easy money available for companies who wanted to make acquisitions. No issuer could sell a new junk bond to anyone!

You can imagine what happened to the stocks of the prospective acquisition candidate "target companies" held by the value managers. Suddenly, there were no hungry corporate acquirers out there to whom they could sell. The values of many of the stocks declined dramatically and these value managers produced relatively poor results for the next two or three years.

Growth — The Next Microsoft

Growth managers are sort of the opposite of value managers. They look for stocks in fast-growing businesses. These are the kinds of companies that can be expected to compound their earnings year after year producing steadily rising earnings per share. We often associate growth with high technology industries like computers and software or biomedical companies, or perhaps, even rapidly growing fast food chains. Managers specializing in those kinds of companies had not done well during the 1980s. The stocks were somewhat neglected while everybody was trying to buy shares of takeover targets.

Shortly after the takeover game ended in 1989, investor interest returned to growth company stocks and growth managers produced stellar results for a few good years. Again, it was not that growth stock managers had sudden flashes of brilliance. It was that the market simply shifted back in their favor.

The shifting back and forth between investment styles as one outperforms the other happens from time to time within our domestic stock market. It occurs in world markets as well. Not only do shifts occur between growth and value styles but between large company stocks, small company stocks, and what are known as mid-cap stocks. Mid-cap is Wall Street-ese for middle-size companies.

Beyond Changing Styles — Global Shifts

If this were not complicated enough, there are other shifts that occur. The global economy is a big place. After World War II, the vast majority of the world's tradeable stocks were those of United States-based companies. Today, U.S. company stocks comprise only about 30 percent of the value of all the stocks traded in the world. Now, in order to take advantage of the opportunities available, one must think globally. There are outstanding companies in Canada, Latin America, Europe, Japan, and the fast-growing Pacific Rim countries.

Not only do we have to think about growth and value and large and small and mid-cap but, now, domestic and foreign. Don't forget bonds, they come in many flavors as well — U. S. Treasury, state and local government, as well as corporate. Bonds can be of high quality, low quality, or medium quality. Bonds can be selected with different maturities and, of course, there are foreign bonds to consider. You

can find mutual funds managed by very good managers who specialize in any of these areas. There are over 4,500 mutual funds from
which to choose today.

To simplify matters, here is a table of investment returns. The
table shows what returns you would have earned on average by investing in one of five different categories of investments over the last
14 years. We have highlighted what would have been the best place
to be in any given year.

TABLE XI*

INVESTMENT RETURNS

YEAR	U.S. STOCKS	FOREIGN STOCKS(1)	PRECIOUS METALS	BONDS	MONEY MARKET FUNDS
1979	18.5%	6.2%	126.5%	2.3%	9.2%
1980	33.3%	24.4%	57.3%	3.3%	12.8%
1981	-5.1%	-1.0%	-25.8%	6.5%	17.1%
1982	21.4%	-0.9%	43.1%	28.9%	12.6%
1983	22.5%	24.6%	-0.5%	8.5%	8.8%
1984	6.1%	7.9%	-26.3%	12.5%	10.1%
1985	31.8%	56.7%	-7.5%	19.4%	7.8%
1986	18.6%	69.9%	37.6%	14.6%	6.4%
1987	4.9%	24.9%	32.0%	1.4%	6.1%
1988	16.6%	28.6%	-19.0%	7.8%	7.1%
1989	32.2%	10.8%	24.8%	11.3%	8.9%
1990	-3.1%	-23.2%	-22.9%	7.0%	7.9%
1991	30.4%	12.5%	-6.0%	15.7%	5.8%
1992	7.6%	-13.9%	-15.4%	6.9%	3.4%
1993	10.1%	32.9%	84.3%	9.8%	2.7%

*Source: *The Handbook For No-Load Investors* 1990-1994 editions

The Right Place At The Right Time

You probably remember the very high inflation rates that we experienced in the United States in the late 1970s and early 1980s. Inflation is very bad for bonds because bond investors, even though earning interest, are rapidly losing purchasing power. As you can see from Table XI, a bond manager, no matter how skilled, could not make much money for his investors in 1979, 1980 or 1981. Interest rates were going up as investors adjusted for more inflation. Remember the seesaw in Chapter Four. Bond prices were dropping like a rock. The poor bond manager was in the wrong place at the wrong time. Investors frightened by inflation during that period wanted to hold anything but bonds. Everybody wanted to buy California real estate, Chinese export porcelain, Oriental rugs, Impressionist paintings, gold coins, or bags of diamonds. Anything was better than holding bonds.

You can see from Table XI, precious metals-related investments soared in value in 1979 and 1980. Any five-year-old presented with a list of fifty gold mining stocks and asked to select ten for investment would have looked like a prodigy a year later. Simply put, the market was in his favor, and he couldn't miss. The five-year-old would have been in the right place at the right time.

Neither the bad bond market nor the great gold market lasted for too many months. It would have taken a very nimble investor, indeed, to shift all of his money from bonds to gold stocks or from bond funds to gold funds to catch the whole trend of the market. Other trends, however, have lasted much longer. The exceptional performance of foreign stock markets and mutual funds investing in foreign stocks lasted for quite a while, from 1985 through 1988. Clearly, an investor looking at the track record of foreign mutual funds from the vantage point of 1989 would have thought it a no-brainer to invest all her money in foreign funds. She probably would have been encouraged to do that by the "pop finance" on the covers of magazines seen at the check-out line in the supermarket. Article after article would have highlighted the mutual funds with the best five-year track records, and none would have told the unsuspecting investor that the underlying causes for the trend were about over.

There were good fundamental reasons why foreign funds were a smart investment in 1985, and not in 1989. In the mid-1980s, the United States dollar had risen in value versus most foreign currencies. The high value of the U.S. dollar as opposed to foreign currencies made it very difficult for United States manufacturers to sell their wares in foreign countries. A French contractor who wanted to buy earth moving equipment to build an airport in the Middle East had to come up with a lot more francs to convert into U.S. dollars to buy from Caterpillar than he did if he was converting his francs to yen to buy from Komatsu, the Japanese equivalent of Caterpillar. The Frenchman made the obvious choice and bought the Japanese equipment.

About that time we began to see magazine articles describing the manufacturing heart of the U.S. as the rust belt. Eventually, trade imbalances became so extreme that a meeting was held among the finance ministers who ran the central banks of the seven largest industrialized countries of the world. These finance ministers, from what are called the G-7 countries, agreed with the U.S. that the value of the U.S. dollar had to come down relative to other world currencies to try to redress the trade imbalances. When this plan was publicly announced, there was much nay-saying by the financial press. Learned economists asserted that the central banks didn't have enough economic power to depress the value of the U.S. dollar. They did. These powerful central banks are perfectly capable of producing such a result by manipulating interest rates. The dollar declined against the major foreign currencies, the pound, the yen, and the franc. U.S. manufactured goods again became competitively priced in the world market place.

If you were holding foreign stocks that were trading overseas and denominated in foreign currencies, you made not only a profit from your stock investments but it was greatly magnified when you translated your appreciating foreign currency back into U.S. dollars. This trend went on for quite a while, ending in 1989. There was plenty of time to take advantage of it.

This sounds like a very complicated trend to climb aboard. If in 1985, you had called your local stockbrokers and told them you wanted to buy some British or French or Japanese stocks, they would have probably thought you were crazy. Since commissions were involved, they might have even tried to sell you some. Think how much simpler it would have been to allocate a portion of your portfolio to a no-load diversified foreign fund run by an experienced manager, letting her or him do the stock picking.

Use Funds To Benefit From Global And Domestic Trends

I don't mean to oversimplify this idea of using no-load mutual funds to capitalize on trends either around the globe or within U.S. domestic markets. Trends are much easier to see looking backward than looking forward. Rarely, will you get in precisely at the beginning or out exactly at the end. As Bernard Baruch the early twentieth century financier said, "Only liars do that". It obviously demands that you do your homework and be willing to constantly monitor your portfolio.

This is an incredibly powerful concept. The ability to buy and sell no-load mutual funds, in effect, moving money from one expert manager to another in anticipation of changing markets gives investors like you and I a decided advantage over large institutional investors who do not have the flexibility to hire and fire portfolio managers in any kind of short time frame.

Timers vs. Asset Allocators

To show you how powerful the concept really is, *Investor's Business Daily* published a study done by CDA\Wiesenberger in its annual volume "Investment Companies". The study first appeared in 1975 and was later updated through September 30, 1992.

The study is based on two fictitious investors. Both are truly gifted. Mr. Timer can perfectly call every stock market swing of at least 10 percent, while Ms. Allocator chooses among energy, financial services, gold, health care, technology, and utility stocks and can tell which sector will do better in a given year.

Both investors begin with $1,000 on January 1, 1980. By September 30, 1992, Mr. Timer our perfect timer, had called nine major market turns and parlayed his $1,000 to $14,650. Meanwhile, by picking each year's top-performing sector, Ms. Allocator turned her $1,000 into $62,640. By comparison, a $1,000 buy and hold investment in the Standard & Poor's 500 Stock Index would have grown to $6,030.

According to Steve Savage, managing editor at CDA\Wiesenberger, the magnitude of the difference between timing and industry allocation is even more powerful in the original 1975 study.

In the original study, Mr. Timer who started in 1940 with $1,000 made 12 perfect market calls and had $104,761 by the end of 1974. The original Ms. Allocator who was granted more liberal powers that allowed her to move among dozens of industries made 29 investments and turned her $1,000 into more than $11 million.

Both examples are clearly impossible, but Savage notes that the examples do indicate that good selection, which real life managers have demonstrated is possible, is more important than timing. Most students of financial markets have concluded that perfect timing is un-achievable.

CHAPTER EIGHT

PORTFOLIO STRATEGY — NOBODY IS QUITE LIKE ME

Markets change, tastes change, so the companies and individuals who choose to compete in those markets must change.
— *Dr. An Wang*

Everybody's Different — What Do You Want?

All investors have different investment objectives. Some have very long-term investment horizons and are willing to accept a lot of risk. Remember, by risk I don't mean risk of loss, I mean volatility. They don't care if their portfolio fluctuates up and down in any given year. They know that if they invest in funds with growth objectives, the market statistics will work for them, and eventually, they will make a lot of money. That's all a function of compound interest.

We are often called upon to manage retirement accounts for young professionals. A forty-year-old earning several hundred thousand dol-

"HIS MAKES ALL MY PROBLEMS SEEM PRETTY
NSIGNIFICANT, EXCEPT, OF COURSE, FOR MY
NVESTMENT PORTFOLIO."

lars per year will want to make maximum contributions to her retirement plan every year. She is not going to be concerned that one bad
market year her retirement account may be down 10, 15, or maybe
even 20 percent. She knows she has plenty of time to make up the
difference. If our young professional sets aside $22,500 a year, the
current allowable limit for contributions into tax-free retirement accounts for the next 30 years, until she is seventy-years-old, she is
going to have a substantial retirement fund. If the contributions can
be made to grow at 12 percent a year, the long-term historic average
for smaller company stocks, then she will accumulate $5,400,000 by
the time she retires. If, on the other hand, she is cautious and elects
to keep her money in what she considers very safe intermediate-
term U.S. Treasury bonds, yielding an average of five percent, she will
wind up with only $1,500,000.

Our professional will, no doubt, choose the more aggressive
course of action, and it clearly makes sense for her to do so. Her
retirement portfolio should contain an array of funds, both foreign
and domestic and they should be managed opportunistically to take
advantage of trends in the marketplace.

Remember our vigorous eighty-year-old widow Elizabeth from
Chapter Three. She was fortunate enough to have the large New York
bank managing her trust disagree with her husband 20 years ago
when he wanted all her money invested in bonds. By investing half
in a diversified portfolio of quality stocks, the bank produced far
better results for her.

Elizabeth has some other investment funds. About five years ago,
her three children, none of whom are investment professionals, asked
us to take over the management of this money. Considering her age
and need for current income, as well as the composition of her other
assets, we developed a portfolio strategy for her. Twenty-five percent
of her available funds were invested in an actively managed no-load
mutual fund portfolio with a growth objective. Remember, her mother

lived to be 98 and it is likely that she has a very long future. The stock mutual funds' purpose is to protect Elizabeth from the eroding effects of inflation.

The balance of Elizabeth's money was invested in mutual funds containing very long-term, high-grade corporate bonds. The bond funds pay monthly interest that she can spend for living expenses. Long maturity bond funds were chosen to take advantage of what we perceived at the time to be an impending decline in long-term interest rates. Interest rates did decline, and remember the seesaw in Chapter Four, the net asset value of her bond fund shares rose substantially.

Fund Types As Building Blocks

Mutual funds each have their own clearly stated objectives. The Investment Company Institute, which serves as a trade association for mutual fund companies, has broken down about twenty different classes of funds grouped by objective. They are included in Appendix B. The possible combinations of types of mutual funds are almost endless, and an appropriate portfolio can be designed to fit almost any investor's financial objectives.

How Do You Select Funds?

When we build a portfolio for an investor, we select funds from a broad universe that we have already pre-screened, based on a number of criteria.

Who Is Best? Peer Group Comparisons

First of all, funds should have performed well over at least the last two or three years when measured against other funds with the same objectives. By looking at funds within specific objective categories, such as those with capital appreciation objectives and value style managements, we can compare managers' records. That will pre-identify attractive funds that we can use in the event that one day we will want to move some of our money to a fund managed with such a value style.

Is The Person Who Picked The Stocks Still There?

The next thing we look for is continuity of management. A fund may have a fine two- or three-year track record when measured against its peer group. But if the person who made the profitable decisions retired, or left the fund six months ago, we have no idea what the new manager is going to be able to do going forward. This is particularly critical when looking at funds managed by some of the smaller fund management companies who do not have enormous staffs. Where management companies have big staffs, such as those found in large organizations like Fidelity, the shifting of managers doesn't seem to make as much difference in fund performance.

How About Big vs. Little Funds?

We pay a lot of attention to the size of the fund. From time to time you will see compilations of funds' performance printed in newspapers and magazines. It is not unusual in those lists to find some obscure funds whose names are unfamiliar, even to those of us who pursue this full time. In any given year, some little fund with two or three million dollars in assets invested in only a few stocks will hit a home run, and one of its stocks will triple or quadruple or go up by a factor of 10 or 20. Statistically, that will vault the fund to the top of the list. We ignore those. They are too small and too erratic to be used in seriously managed portfolios.

There is a theory that small, not tiny, funds perform better. The theory makes a lot of sense. Smaller funds are more flexible and if their performance begins to attract a lot of new money, they may well use it to purchase more of the stocks they already hold. If they are small company stocks with thin markets, this buying may actually push up their prices. We have noticed deterioration in fund performance as they get very large, but this is by no means always the case.

How Important Are Long-Term Track Records?

You will often read that you should select funds based on track records. Tables of five- and 10-year performance appear with regularity in magazines and in mutual fund advertising. The uninformed investor assumes "if it did well in the past, it will probably do OK in the future".

We know from our discussion of the importance of a manager being in the right place at the right time that past performance may not be of much use in predicting future performance under different market conditions. Obviously, the same thing holds true for mutual funds.

Burt Berry, who publishes the **NoLOAD FUND *X* newsletter, periodically does studies on the usefulness of long-term records to predict future fund performance. In January 1990, Burt noted, in a newsletter column entitled "Are Long-Term Records Predictive? Not Very." that,

Each year we report our ongoing study dating back to the five years ending 1971. We review performance of the top 25 funds in each five-year period to see how they fared in the following year and in the following five years. 1989 was no exception to the pattern in which few, if any, of the top 25 repeat. From the 12/79 - 12/84 period, none of the top 25 were in the top 25 in the following years. Only four of the twenty five winners were even in the top 100 in the following five years.

How did the top 25 from the five years 12/83 - 12/88 do the next year, 1989? One fund made the top 25 in 1989. Only two of the 25 ranked in the top 100 in 1989. Only nine of the top 25 were even in the top 500 in 1989.

Are there other professions where the thrill of victory is so often followed by the agony of defeat? So much for predictability.

Portfolio Strategy

To simplify things, let's confine our portfolio strategy discussion to stock mutual fund portfolios where our objectives are long-term growth with moderate risk. We find that the vast majority of our clients are interested in that kind of investing rather than either maximum aggressive or very conservative approaches. The same general technique that we use with stock funds applies to bond fund portfolios as well.

The Heart Of The Portfolio

Our approach is to try to build a core position in the portfolio, perhaps as much as 60 percent, from high-quality, large-company, U.S., and foreign, stock funds. The foreign and domestic mix will depend on our view of where in their economic and stock market cycles the U.S. and other foreign countries may be. Countries with declining interest rates, moderate inflation, and good prospects for growth are obviously going to be more attractive for stock investments than countries faced with rising interest rates, rising inflation, and overheated economies. Sometimes, these core positions are going to be weighted heavily toward domestic funds when we are optimistic about the U.S. economy and its prospects. Other times, we will use heavier weightings of diversified foreign funds if overseas economic prospects and economic conditions call for it. Think of these core positions as funds that we expect to hold for a long time, continually monitoring them against competitive funds to be sure that they are performing in line with our expectations. They will go up or down with the foreign and domestic stock markets and changing currency relationships, but they should do better than the average of their peer group.

Adding Spice To The Mix

We will often break the balance of the portfolio up into small blocks. The idea is to be more opportunistic with pieces of the portfolio, buying small amounts of more volatile funds that we expect to be very profitable. Who is in the right place at the right time? These are the judgments that are perhaps the most demanding but that can also make the most difference in overall investment performance. If we believe that one group of companies or an industry is likely to benefit greatly from some change going on in the economy, we will move some money to a fund invested in that market segment.

Investments made in health care stock funds around the end of the 1980s are a good example of opportunistic segment investing. At that time, the takeover era had effectively ended, there was a general perception that the U.S. economy was headed into recession. Investors were interested in finding companies that could still grow and produce rising earnings under those circumstances. Health care stocks seemed to be a likely beneficiary. Sensing this, we began making small investments in what was then known as Financial Programs Strategic Health Sciences Portfolio. We continually added to the positions as the trend accelerated. In 1991, the fund actually gained about 90 percent.

You can imagine that even if you only have 10 percent of your portfolio in something that goes up 90 percent in a year, it is going to have a large effect on your total return. Assuming the rest of the portfolio went up 10 percent and that this block went up 90 percent, your total return for the year would be 18 percent. Finding a 90 percent gainer is extraordinarily rare, but it is not unusual to find some 20 and 30 percent gainers in years when the broad market produces more average returns.

Incidentally, our clients' investment in the Health Sciences Fund was sold early in 1992 when we saw the political rhetoric heating up before the Presidential campaign. Clearly, medical technology and pharmaceutical companies were going to become the target of politically inspired criticism. We thought the stocks would be unlikely to continue to advance, and would probably decline under governmental threats of more regulation and price controls.

Later that year, thinking the threat had largely been reflected in the price of the stocks and that they had been driven down to bargain levels, we bought into the area again. The investment went nowhere. We sold it and went on to better things. You can imagine how costly following this strategy would have been had we attempted to do this with high-commission load funds.

Return Enhancement

We call this strategy of building core positions and then trying to raise average returns by using more specialized funds, a return enhancement approach. This approach gives you the opportunity to let long-term history work in your favor on the broad middle part of your portfolio while you are more adventuresome at the margin. The strategy is not a "hot money" strategy that attempts to achieve performance in one year equal to the "hottest" high performing fund. Obviously, the only way to do that is to put all the money in one fund and it has to be the right one. Taking such an un-diversified approach would invite disaster! The strategy gives you the opportunity, without taking too much risk, to make investments in some more narrow, specialized areas of the market. We use these specialized funds when our analysis and judgment of the market say there are clear opportunities for a fund manager who devotes his attention to those specific areas to be in the right place at the right time.

Sector Funds

There are lots of specialty funds. Within the mutual fund industry they are known as "sector" funds. There are many sectors such as computers and software, health care, home finance, regional banks, metal and mining, and so forth. There are other funds that specialize in foreign country investing. If you like the prospects for the Mexican stock market, you can allocate money to a proven portfolio manager who spends all of his time researching and trading Mexican stocks. You can do the same thing if you want to allocate some money to the fast-growing economies of the Pacific Rim, i.e. Hong Kong, Singapore, Malaysia, et al, countries that should benefit from the enormous growth in China as it converts to a more free market economy.

We could go on with many more examples of using narrow specialized funds. But I want to make it clear that in managing a portfolio of this type, you must continually stay on top of events that can create or change trends in the worldwide financial markets. You cannot be an expert in everything. That is why you leave the individual stock selections up to experts. You must attempt to understand the big changes that effect the investment world.

Grasping The Very, Very Big Picture - Taxes

Who would have guessed that the major change in the U.S. tax code at the beginning of the 1980s which eventually reduced personal income tax rates to a maximum of about 28 percent, from previous marginal rates of around 70 percent, would have had so many far-reaching effects on the U.S. economy?

Suddenly, high-yield corporate bonds, "junk", became attractive to us as investors. If we could buy junk bonds paying 15 percent interest and only pay a 28 percent tax on the income we would still wind up with 10.8 percent in our pocket. (If we had a $1,000 bond it would pay us $150 per year. At our new lower 28 percent tax rate, our tax would be $42. That would leave us $108 after taxes, or a 10.8 percent after tax return on our $1,000 investment.) Why go to all the trouble of trying to find growth stocks when those kinds of returns were available? Out of this change in the tax code, and the public's resulting appetite for high-yield bond mutual funds, came the take-over era of the 1980s. It was these bonds, sold to the high-yield fund managers, that financed much of the decade's tremendous surge in merger activity. If we had understood the full, long-term effect of Reagan's tax reductions, we would have placed all of our money with value-style money managers, who were buying stocks in takeover targets. We would have enjoyed years of tremendous gains as the takeover era unfolded.

The change in the income tax code had other ramifications. It no longer made sense to buy a huge house and carry an enormous mort-gage. A couple's $4,000 per month mortgage payment, virtually all deductible for federal income tax purposes, only cost them $1,200 per month after taxes when they were 70 percent tax bracket payers. When tax rates were cut to 28 percent, the same couple's actual costs after taxes jumped to $2,880, more than doubling. Is it any wonder that housing inflation died? Large houses, second homes, and big boats which also qualified as homes under the tax code languished on the market in the late 1980s.

In 1993, the Federal Income Tax Code was changed again, and marginal tax rates for high income earners went over 40 percent, even substantially higher than that for people who lived in high-tax states. Federal capital gains rates remained at 28 percent. Wouldn't you expect with the shift in the tax structure, investors would shift their attention to the pursuit of long-term capital gains? Perhaps the shares of smaller, fast-growing companies will benefit. Who needs utility dividends taxed at over 40 percent when they can get capital gains taxed at 28 percent?

It always takes a long time for all the ramifications of a change in the tax code to work their way through the economy. These longer-term effects fall under the "law of unintended consequences" and are usually not fully thought out by Congress when they change the tax code.

How Do You Spot Developing Trends?

What techniques can you use to spot these trends as they begin to unfold and reflect in the financial markets? Something needs to bring them to your attention so that you can determine for yourself whether or not these trends promise to continue.

With the large universe of mutual funds available today, one approach is to watch for changes in relative performance between groups of funds. If you have a home computer, there are software packages available that do relative strength analysis, measuring fund group performance one against the other. If it appears, for instance, that growth funds are beginning to outperform value funds in the U.S. stock market, you can ask yourself if there are underlying fundamental reasons. There was a very clear reason why it was happening at the end of the 1980s. You will recall our discussion of the end of the takeover era. Given those circumstances, it made sense to move your money from funds managed by value managers to funds managed by growth managers.

In a more narrow sense, in early 1990, it became clear that sector funds investing in the health area and in the technology area were beginning to outperform other types of investments. If you understood the fundamental shift of investors' attention back to growth stocks, you could feel reasonably comfortable moving some of your money into funds investing in those areas.

Don't Pay Attention To "Blips"

Short periods of exceptional performance by a narrow specialized group of funds may not have the kind of strong fundamental underpinnings you are looking for. In the past, we have seen funds specializing in gold and precious metal stocks make quick run-ups in value, only to fall back into lackluster performance in a disappointingly short period of time. We have not found a long-term, fundamental change in the economy which justifies making major investments in that area. A real, not imagined, resurgence of inflation could change our minds.

This Approach Is New

The techniques that I am describing to you were virtually unheard of 10 or 15 years ago. There were not many mutual funds available. You could not easily find much detailed statistical history describing their performance. Communications had not yet undergone the revolution we have seen in the last few years.

Fifteen years ago, if you wanted financial information on what the stock market was doing today or what had happened overnight in the Japanese stock market or what the bond market was doing, you had to call your broker. He could probably find out — if not from information available in his branch, at least by calling his New York headquarters. The large brokerage firms had a lock on financial information flows to people like you and me. Telecommunications has changed all that. If you sit home one day with a bad cold and watch CNBC, you will be deluged with financial information from all the world's markets and commentaries from a wide variety of economists, money managers — frauds and geniuses of all persuasions.

You probably will know more about what is going on than your stock-broker who is busy making sales calls all day.

This information explosion combined with the enormous array of choices available, has made it possible for any serious student of the financial markets who is willing to devote the time and energy required, to do a credible job managing his or her investments.

Am I Cut Out To Be A Do-It-Yourself Investor?

When confronted with an investment problem, be it the rollover of money from a previous employer's retirement plan into an IRA, investing an inheritance, or life insurance proceeds, or beginning a serious effort to start saving for your retirement or your children's education, you have a major decision to make. "Should I do it myself? Should I try to do it with a conventional stockbroker, or is there some-where else I can turn?"

The answer to the question depends on how comfortable you are with making and carrying out your own investment strategy. Your success probably depends as much on psychology as on knowledge and intelligence.

Am I Emotionally Suited To Investing My Own Money? Can I Take A Loss?

We find in dealing with clients that they can be their own worst enemies when they try to manage their investments. It is not unusual to have a client come to us as Ginger did. She's a very bright woman who manages the business aspects of her husband's practice. She has had poor results in trying to manage both the practice's retirement plans and the couple's own personal savings. Her husband has no interest in finance or investments. He loves taking care of his pa-tients and is totally involved with helping them. Ginger has taken the sole responsibility for their financial affairs.

As we analyzed Ginger's portfolio, we found some sensible investments, a few no-load mutual funds, and a few high-quality bonds. We also found some relatively large positions in stocks that had been bought at high prices a couple of years before. Typically, they were those that had received a lot of publicity. Victimized by pop finance she had bought the stocks at the peak of their popularity and had held them while they dropped dramatically. When asked why she had not sold them, she replied, "I can't sell them because I would lose money. I'll keep them until they get back to what I paid for them." She was telling us that she could not psychologically take a loss. It was this inability to take small losses when her investments didn't work out that had ruined her portfolio returns when small losses deteriorated into big losses.

This inability to take a loss on an investment is not unusual. We have frequently had clients tell us that they hire us to get around their own shortcomings in this area. Everybody has some losses if they invest. Nobody bats 100 percent. It is critical that the losses be recognized and dealt with.

Can I Control My Spending?

We have clients who know that they need to save money for a child's college education or for retirement who simply cannot keep themselves from spending money if it is too readily available to them. We all know that once we distance ourselves from our money by depositing it into an IRA account or some other tax-advantaged retirement fund, we never think about pulling it back out and spending it for a trip, or a car, or an oriental rug. If the money is in our checking account, the temptation is sometimes irresistible. Simply put, some clients hire investment advisors to psychologically distance themselves from their money. If someone else is managing it, they don't consider it spendable, so they don't spend it!

Am I Really Patient?

Some people don't have the patience to let the market work for them. They expect too much, too quickly, when they make their own investments. They are really not investors, but are market timers and gamblers. In this age of instant gratification, they somehow expect their stock to go up on Wednesday just because they bought it on Tuesday. Taking an intense daily interest in investments leaves them vulnerable to being buffeted day-to-day by the effects on the market of news, of opinions, and of pop finance. Investors caught in this trap may have a good idea, but they get tired of waiting for it to come to fruition. As opposed to the philosophy of never selling until a small loss turns into a big disaster, these are the ones who sell too soon. You will often hear them say, "Gee, that's a great stock, I used to own some but it seemed like it was never going to do anything, so I sold it." These are the kind of people who seem to have an easier time transferring their anxieties over to us and letting us be patient for them.

Am I A Gambler At Heart?

We understand gamblers. Even though I know better, I too feel an overwhelming urge to go for a double or a triple every once in a while. People who like to speculate in stocks should establish two different pools of investment money. The larger pool should be for serious long-term investments. The smaller pool can be used to try for those doubles and triples. That way, a few losing bets can't ruin their overall investment program. Who knows, you might hit a triple. What fun that would be!

Am I Really "Into" This Stuff?

As a practical matter, most people just don't have the time, the patience, the educational background, or the interest to get deeply involved in dealing with investments every day. They have businesses to run, carpools to drive, the hungry to feed, or families to care for.

Partially because of the information explosion, coupled with the significant changes in the securities business, a new and as yet largely unrecognized industry has emerged: Registered Investment Advisory Firms, working for fees rather than for commissions. Once such firms were only available to the very wealthy. Now they are beginning to displace old-time stockbrokers and bank trust departments as the place smaller investors can turn for help.

Investment advisors

"DEAR, WHY DON'T YOU JUST WATCH 'GILLIGAN'S ISLAND'?"

CHAPTER NINE

THE NEW BREED OF INVESTMENT ADVISOR

The first-rate man will try to surround himself with his equals, or betters if possible. The second-rate man will surround himself with third-rate men. The third-rate man will surround himself with fifth-rate men. — *Andre Weil*

This new type of registered investment advisor is dedicated to working with investors with moderate-size portfolios, or with small companies in the management of their retirement plan assets. These financial advisory firms are not commission-driven like stockbrokers, but instead are paid on a fee basis like CPAs or attorneys. Investment advisors typically work with clients who have from $100,000 to $200,000, up to perhaps, $10,000,000 — an area not previously of interest to the very large institutional money managers. Typically, accounts of that size have not been well-managed by stockbrokers and bank trust departments.

What's A Registered Investment Advisor?

The term "Registered Investment Advisor" should give you only a minimal amount of comfort. Make sure any firm you work with is registered with the Federal Securities & Exchange Commission and, if required, with your state's regulatory authorities. The Investment Advisory Act of 1940 basically said that anyone not licensed as a broker who gives financial advice for a fee has to be registered under the Act. The Act imposes some regulatory requirements, such as how long records and files must be maintained and lays out what facts about the advisor or the firm must be disclosed to clients. Advisors file reports with the government each year to keep their registration in effect. You are entitled to copies of those forms and should always ask for them and read them. They are called ADV forms. The Act further protects you from certain kinds of deceptive advertising and other practices that would not be in your best interest.

At the federal level, there is, unfortunately, no educational requirement, no test, and limited auditing of advisory firms. The average advisory firm, based on the government's current schedule, can expect to be audited by the Securities & Exchange Commission only about once every 27 years. Firms upon whom complaints have been filed can expect to be audited much more frequently. Some states have much more stringent requirements, including bonding, testing, etc.

The Registered Investment Advisory designation is something you should look for as it affords you some protection. It does not mean that the registered advisor is a competent investor. You need to determine that on a case-by-case basis. Occasionally, you will run across a stockbroker with Registered Investment Advisor on his calling card. He is hoping it will impress you. It shouldn't.

What Is A Planner?

Do not confuse registered investment advisors with financial planners. Some may have both designations, Registered Investment Advisor and Certified Financial Planner. Planners are usually more like accountants, and in fact, some large accounting firms have partners dedicated to the planning function. There was a lot of work for planners before the 1986 Federal Tax Code changes. Prior to that time, they were usually engaged in assisting people in avoiding or deferring taxes. You will remember, those were the days when there were lots of different kinds of tax shelters, and every high-income professional seemed to be invested up to his or her ears in office buildings and apartments. These made great tax shelters, but often turned out to be very poor investments.

Today due to changes in the tax code that have closed such loopholes, there is a lot less tax planning work done. Planners are most often involved in assisting people with establishing budgets, considering whether or not to buy life insurance, and working on retirement or estate plans. Many planners are dependent on commission income from the sale of insurance products, tax-deferred annuities, and load mutual funds. If you are dealing with a planner be sure you understand how he or she is compensated. You are much better off paying an hourly rate for planning help and then getting unbiased advice when it comes to making investment decisions.

You will see a lot of planners who have the designation CFP. That is a meaningful designation which stands for Certified Financial Planner. The CFP designation signifies that the planner has taken an examination, ascribes to a code of ethics, and meets continuing education requirements which cover many facets of personal finance and estate planning.

Everybody Wants To Be Certified

"Certified" seems to be a handle that everybody wants these days. I suppose that it all started with Certified Public Accountants. That is a respected and well-regulated designation that is meaningful to most people. Trying to piggyback that aura of respectability, other professionals, some not so professional, have tried to figure out ways to add "certified" to their titles. You will find them among planners, security analysts, life insurance sales people, and real estate people. Some of the designations such as Certified Financial Planner are meaningful, many are not. You and I could get together, form an association, and award ourselves the title "Certified Chicken Salad Specialist." We could then put CSS on our cards. Remember, a "certified" title does not necessarily demonstrate that someone is competent at managing money.

Where Did This "New Breed" Of Investment Advisors Come From?

Registered Investment Advisors are not typical financial planning firms. A little history will help you understand why investment advisory firms are emerging to serve smaller investors.

The Break-Up Of Information Monopolies

Only in the last 10 to 15 years, has timely financial information become readily available and affordable to smaller practitioners. You will recall that in years past the large Wall Street brokerage houses controlled the information flow of market information. If we needed information, we had to call a broker. Growing up, I never saw a ticker tape in anyone's den. For those of you younger than I, the ticker tape was a little strip of paper tape that came out of a machine that printed stock quotes on it just as that information was transmitted from the stock exchanges by telegraph to remote locations. Obsolete today, I wonder what they use for ticker tape parades in New York?

Today, with a personal computer, it is possible to access market information not only from the world's stock exchanges, but from the commodity exchanges as well, all in the comfort of your living room. All the late breaking financial news is available at your fingertips. This disintegration of the Wall Street information monopolies is one factor that has allowed the formation of independent advisory firms.

The Discount Brokers Appear

The second revolutionary change goes back to May 1, 1975 when fixed rate commissions for trading stocks on the major stock exchanges were abolished. Prior to the end of that practice, if you wanted to buy 100 shares of General Motors stock, you paid the same commission no matter which brokerage house executed the order and some stockbroker collected his piece of the transaction fee. You paid the broker whether you needed his investment advice or not!

Ending the fixed brokerage commission structure created an opportunity for entrepreneurs to open discount brokerages. They realized that there was a certain knowledgeable portion of the investing public that made their own purchase and sales decisions without help. For those people, being able to trade stocks and bonds cheaply made a lot of sense.

As the discount brokerage firms began to grow and gain public acceptance, they began to offer more comprehensive services, more account insurance, and computerized customer statements that were the equivalent of those being offered by the large full service brokerage firms. During this expansion of services, the discount brokerages were able to keep their costs in check. Without expensive research departments, economists, and printing plants churning out sales material to support very expensive commission sales people, they had an enormous advantage.

Full-Service Brokers Shoot Themselves In The Foot

At the same time that the discount brokerage business was developing, its growth was unintentionally aided by the conventional stockbrokerage business. The old-line, full-service brokerage business seemed to go on a real binge of selling inappropriate products. Lots of limited partnerships were hastily put together with almost total disregard for their underlying economic viability. They were sold to unsuspecting investors and a large proportion of them turned out to be virtually worthless. There were a myriad of other similar abuses reported widely in the press. A rising public skepticism about commissioned stockbrokers sent hordes of investors to the discounters, where they were not subject to sales pressure.

The customers who first gravitated to discount brokers were independent sorts. These kinds of customers were the same type of investors who, on their own, or through small advertisements in financial publications, had discovered and were investing in no-load mutual funds.

Growth Of No-Load Mutual Fund Investing

Twenty years ago investing in no-load mutual funds was a cumbersome process. Prospective investors like you and I would have to find an ad for the fund somewhere and then write off to get a prospectus. Upon receiving the prospectus, if you elected to invest in the fund, you would fill out account opening forms, and send them along with your check to the fund management company that would deposit your check. Then you'd have to wait until they were sure the funds were good before they would purchase your fund shares for you. When you eventually wanted to redeem your shares, you normally notified the fund in writing and they sent you back the appropriate form. You then took the form to your bank and had your signature guaranteed by a bank officer. You then mailed the form to the fund, they redeemed your shares whatever day your letter reached them, and then they forwarded you a check for the proceeds. An ordeal!

Think how difficult it was to handle the paperwork if you decided to sell your shares in a fund managed from Boston, re-investing half the proceeds in a fund headquartered in Kansas City and half in a fund located in San Francisco. The overwhelming paperwork made the kind of actively managed mutual fund portfolio strategy that we have discussed here impractical, if not impossible. The thought that any small advisory firm might be able to do that for several hundred clients was totally impossible. No small firm could afford the enormous clerical staff it would need to take care of all of the paperwork.

Eureka! Trading No-Load Fund Shares

In 1984, Charles Schwab & Co., one of the pioneers in the discount brokerage business, introduced a service aimed at no-load mutual fund investors. Schwab had made arrangements with a handful of funds which allowed it to take customer orders for purchases and sales of the no-load mutual fund shares in the same way it was handling stock transactions. The mutual fund share purchases and sales transactions were handled for very small Schwab fees that were virtually inconsequential for these investors. The advantages to the no-load mutual fund buyer were extensive. No longer did they have to deal directly with the funds through the time-intensive mail process. With one phone call, the investors could sell their Boston mutual fund shares and arrange for the re-investment of the proceeds in mutual funds in Kansas City and San Francisco the following afternoon. Not only that, at the end of each month, all of their holdings would be clearly spelled out on one brokerage statement rather than on many statements, one from each mutual fund company.

The Birth Of An Industry

Schwab was intent on making no-load fund investing easy and inexpensive for investors. He probably didn't recognize it at the time, but this confluence of events — the ready availability of financial data at reasonable cost, the low transaction costs of dealing with discount brokers, the growing public dissatisfaction with commissioned stockbrokers, and the ability to efficiently trade no-load mutual fund shares for multiple clients — was creating a new industry. Still, in 1987, in its infancy, there were less than 100 registered investment advisors employing these strategies trading through Schwab for clients. At that time, we have subsequently been told by Schwab, advisors trading through Schwab had only about $500,000,000 under management. As of the end of 1993, approximately 4,300 independent advisory firms were managing more than $22.9 billion through Schwab for clients. Other discount brokerage firms such as Jack White, Waterhouse Securities, and Fidelity, through their brokerage divisions, also domicile assets for investment advisors, so today's total is even larger.

This growth of investment advisory firms serving individuals, smaller companies, and charitable foundations has occurred simultaneously with the enormous growth of the mutual fund industry. From 1985 to 1993, dollars invested in no-load stock and bond mutual funds have grown from $332 billion to $1.1 trillion. Today there are approximately 2,241 no-load funds. In 1964, there were 50. Part of this growth can be attributed to the early 90s decline in interest rates which made savings accounts and bank CDs unattractive to investors. Surprisingly, while it is common wisdom that this is where the growth has come from, it doesn't completely explain the phenomenon.

Changing Demographics — Aging Boomers

There is a major demographic change occurring in our population. The baby boomers born in the late 1940s and 1950s are aging and reaching their peak earning years. To boomers, retirement is changing from the once abstract concept of "what old folks do when they quit working", to the inevitability that boomers too are going to get there. Today, there is an enormous group of these people in their 40s and early-50s who are beginning to invest seriously for the future. They are putting money aside regularly. Many of them have recognized that they are ill-equipped to manage their money. They have decided it is better professionally managed. Many have chosen mutual funds as the best investment vehicle. Rather than choosing funds for themselves, a number have gravitated to investment advisors because of their fund knowledge and active management skills.

How Do You Find An Investment Advisor?

If you think that an investment advisor is at least worth considering, how do you find one? You could ask your friends. You could try the Yellow Pages. Another way is to walk into a discount brokerage office and ask the manager if their firm deals with any investment advisors. They probably do. Ask for information. The manager will probably be reluctant to recommend a specific advisor, but might mention a couple of firms. Remember, the discount brokers do business with a number of different investment advisors and don't want to make investment advisors angry by appearing to recommend one over another. Further, many firms have restrictions on what their employees can recommend. Some prohibit their employees from even giving out lists of advisors. In spite of such company policies, employees want to be helpful and will frequently give you some informal guidance. Don't try this in a conventional commission-driven stockbrokerage office or you are going to get the broker who, like the automobile sales person, has floor duty that day.

Who Are The People In The Advisory Firm?

When you interview investment advisory firms, you are going to find that their principals come from all sorts of different financially related backgrounds. Some are ex-stockbrokers — those who have come to realize that they cannot serve two masters, both the brokerage firm and their client's best interest. Others may have been trained in the investment arm of banks or insurance companies and have decided to strike out on their own. The firm you choose should have been around for at least a few years and should have a record of investment results to show you.

Make Sure They Are "Fee-Only"

It is important here that you make sure that you are dealing with what is known as a "fee-only" firm. Fee-only means that the only place the firm will be generating revenue is from the fees that you pay them for the work they do for you. They must not earn commissions for what they do for you.

Be Careful Where Your Money Is Held

Never allow an investment advisory firm to hold your money. Most will not, even if you ask them to, as it creates a whole new level of government regulatory burden for them. All legitimate advisory firms will arrange for your assets to be placed in a safe depository such as with a discount broker or a bank or trust company. Most scams that you read about when crooked investment advisors run off with other peoples' money occur because proper asset custodians were not used. Make sure that the investment advisor has no affiliation with the custodian and doesn't share in any custody fees. There are no custody fees involved with discount brokerage accounts. We prefer them to bank custody arrangements that charge you fees for which you receive nothing of real value.

If you pick an investment advisor, it is likely that his recommended custodian will be a discount brokerage firm. He will assist you in opening an account in your name where your assets will be held. Your securities will be safe. All brokers are required to have SIPC insurance (Securities Investor Protection Corporation) and most have additional coverage. The advisor will not have the right to get money out of your account except for the small amount used to pay his management fee. He will have limited powers which allow him to give the discount broker investment instructions. Investment advisors can also manage money held in banks and trust companies using the same limited powers.

Remember, it is your investment account! You are totally in control of the situation. You can terminate your advisor's limited authority over the account by simply notifying the discount broker that you wish to do so. If your selection of advisor was right in the first place, you will never need to exercise that option. It is comforting to know that you have it. You will receive timely confirmations of all purchases and sales and account statements from the discount broker at the end of every month. You will always know what is going on.

How Do Advisors Get Paid?

Fee-based investment advisors usually base their fees on the dollar value of the assets they are managing in your account. Annual fees are normally between one and two percent of assets under management, depending on the size of the account. Sometimes higher percentage fees, or minimum fees, are charged for smaller accounts because they involve just about as much work as the larger ones. Fees are usually assessed at the end of each calendar quarter when the value of the account is known. If a client had agreed to a 1.33 percent annual fee, the client would be charged .333 of one percent of the assets under management each quarter. If the account were one million dollars, the client would be charged $3,333 for the quarter.

It is not unusual for investment advisors to charge small fees when they open your account.The fee partially compensates them for their consulting time in helping you determine your investment objectives and constructing your initial portfolio.

Check References

Picking an investment advisory firm, other than the pure chemistry of "do I like them and do I think I could work with them?" is going to depend heavily on references.Ask for references from other clients that are in situations similar to yours and talk to them. Find out what they think and whether they are truly satisfied with what the investment advisor is doing for them.

Be Totally Honest With Yourself And Your Advisor

Make sure that your investment advisor really understands your financial situation and your objectives.Don't tell the advisor you want an aggressively managed portfolio if the thought of being down 10 to 15 percent in some particularly rocky month is going to frighten you to death. Don't tell the advisor you are ultra-conservative if down deep inside you want to go for really big gains.The advisor can help you think through your objectives, but in the end, they are yours, and the advisor's job is to try to help you achieve them.

Expect Ups And Downs

If you are a long-term stock mutual fund investor, or if you have a balanced account containing both stock and bond funds, don't expect your account to be up every month. Over long periods of time, the stock market spends about twice as much time going up as it does going down. You can see from the trust account example in Appendix D that even an account that averaged almost 15 percent annually over 5 1/2 years, had 43 up months and 22 down months.

Sometimes you will experience a string of down months or a string of up months. Fluctuations in value are to be expected. Try to accept them with some equanimity. Your investment advisor is being paid to put up with the daily pressure of the markets.

Advisors are very interested in producing the best possible financial results for their clients. That is the way they keep clients. They are going to do everything they can to minimize transaction costs in your account. Using discount brokers is only the first step. Often, a large investment advisory firm can negotiate lower transaction costs for its clients than would normally be available to an individual investor using the same discount brokerage firm.

For an individual investor who is not an investment professional, the use of a competent, fee-only, registered investment advisory firm, specializing in no-load mutual fund portfolio management, seems a winning concept.

One of the strongest cases in support of the use of mutual funds that I have run across appeared in Martin J. Whitman's January 31, 1994 quarterly report on his Third Avenue Value Fund. Whitman wrote,

> An investor in mutual funds is pretty well protected against being wiped out by promoters pedalling phony tax shelters, phony new issues, penny stocks, and over-leveraged margin accounts. The investor in companies regulated under the ICA (Investment Company Act of 1940) is immunized against out and out thievery. Further, because of diversification requirements, limitations on borrowings, and limitations on fees that can be charged, the mutual fund investor is even protected against the stupidity and avarice of advisors to a much greater extent than has existed in any other investment vehicle.

I have little to add and would encourage you to seriously consider Whitman's comments. The investment method that we have discussed here is the result of many years of trial, error and expensively learned lessons. It is your best hope for coping with the investment challenges you face as we move into the 21st century. It can work for you!

APPENDIX A

S&P BOND RATING DEFINITIONS

AAA The highest rating assigned by Standard & Poor's to debt obligations is AAA. The capacity to pay interest and repay principal is extremely high.

AA These bonds have a very strong capacity to pay interest and repay principal and differ only slightly from the highest-rated issues.

A Strong capacity to pay interest and repay principal although these bonds are somewhat more susceptible to the adverse effects of changes in circumstances and economic conditions than more highly rated bonds.

BBB Only an adequate capacity to pay interest and repay principal. Whereas they normally exhibit adequate protection parameters, adverse economic conditions or changing circumstances are more likely to lead to a weakened capacity to pay interest and repay principal for these bonds.

BB, B, CCC, CC These bonds are predominantly speculative. Their capacity to pay interest and repay principal in accordance with the terms of the obligation is substantially lower. BB indicates the lowest degree of speculation and CC the highest degree of speculation.

C This rating is reserved for income bonds on which no interest is being paid.

D Bonds rated D are in default; payment of interest and\or repayment of principal is in arrears.

Plus (+) or Minus (-) The rating from AA to B may be modified by the addition of a plus or minus sign to show relative standing within the major rating categories.

Moody's rating are similar except their grades run: Aaa, Aa, A, Baa, Ba, B, Caa, Ca, C.

In addition many small issues held by the funds are "unrated". This simply means the corporations issuing did not pay to have their bonds rated.

APPENDIX B

MUTUAL FUND INVESTMENT OBJECTIVES

The Investment Company Institute of Washington, D.C. classifies mutual funds in 22 broad categories according to their basic objectives. Here is a brief description of each:

Aggressive Growth Funds seek maximum capital gains as their investment objective. Current income is not a significant factor. Some may invest in stocks of businesses that are somewhat out of the mainstream, such as fledgling companies, new industries, companies fallen on hard times or industries temporarily out of favor. Some may also use specialized investment techniques such as option writing or short-term trading.

Balanced Funds generally have a three-part investment objective: 1) to conserve the investors' initial principal, 2) to pay current income, and 3) to promote long-term growth of both this principal and income. Balanced funds have a portfolio mix of bonds, preferred stocks, and common stocks.

Corporate Bond Funds seek a high level of income by purchasing bonds of corporations for the majority of the fund's portfolio. The rest of the portfolio may be in U.S. Treasury bonds or bonds issued by a federal agency.

Flexible Portfolio Funds may be 100 percent invested in stocks or bonds or money market instruments, depending on market conditions. These funds give the money managers the greatest flexibility in anticipating or responding to economic changes.

Ginnie Mae or GNMA Funds seek a high level of income by investing in mortgage securities backed by the Government National Mortgage Association (GNMA). To qualify for this category, the majority of the portfolio must always be invested in mortgage-backed securities.

Global Bond Funds seek a high level of current income by investing in the debt securities of companies and countries worldwide, including the U.S.

Global Equity Funds seek growth in the value of their investments by investing in securities traded worldwide, including the U.S. Compared to direct investments, global funds offer investors an easier avenue to investing abroad. The funds' professional money managers handle the trading and recordkeeping details and deal with differences in currencies, languages, time zones, laws and regulations, and business customs and practices. In addition to another layer of diversification, global funds add another layer of risk—exchange-rate risk.

Growth and Income Funds invest mainly in the common stock of companies that have had increasing share value but also a solid record of paying dividends. This type of fund attempts to combine long-term capital growth with a steady stream of income.

Growth Funds invest in the common stock of well-established companies. Their primary aim is to produce an increase in the value of their investments (capital gains) rather than a flow of dividends. Investors who buy a growth fund are more interested in seeing the fund's share price rise than in receiving income from dividends.

High-yield Bond Funds maintain at least two thirds of their portfolios in lower-rated corporate bonds (Baa or lower by Moody's rating service and BBB or lower by Standard and Poor's rating service). In return for a generally higher yield, investors must bear a greater degree of risk than for higher-rated bonds.

Income-Bond Funds seek a high level of current income by investing at all times in a mix of corporate and government bonds.

Income-Equity Funds seek a high level of current income by investing primarily in equity securities of companies with good dividend-paying records.

Income-Mixed Funds seek a high level of current income by investing in income-producing securities, including both equities and debt instruments.

International Funds seek growth in the value of their investments by investing in equity securities of companies located outside the U.S. Two thirds of their portfolios must be invested at all times to be categorized here.

National Municipal Bond Funds—Long-term invest in bonds issued by states and municipalities to finance schools, highways, hospitals, airports, bridges, water and sewer works, and other public projects. In most cases, income earned on these securities is not taxed by the federal government but may be taxed under state and local laws. For some taxpayers, portions of income earned on these securities may be subject to the federal alternative minimum tax.

Precious Metals\Gold Funds seek an increase in the value of their investments by investing at least two thirds of their portfolios in securities associated with gold, silver, and other precious metals.

State Municipal Bond Funds—Long-term work just like national municipal bond funds (see above) except their portfolios contain the issues of only one state. A resident of that state has the advantage of receiving income free of both federal and state tax. For some taxpayers, portions of income from these securities may be subject to the federal alternative minimum tax.

Taxable Money Market Mutual Funds seek to maintain a stable net asset value by investing in the short-term, high-grade securities sold in the money market. These are generally the safest, most stable securities available and include Treasury Bills, certificates of deposit of large banks, and commercial paper (the short-term IOUs of large U.S. corporations). Money market funds limit the average maturity of their portfolio to 90 days or less.

Tax-exempt Money Market Funds—National invest in municipal securities with relatively short maturities. Investors who use these funds seek investments with minimum risk. For some taxpayers, portions of income from certain of these securities may be subject to the federal alternative minimum tax.

Tax-exempt Money Market Funds—State work just like other tax-exempt money market funds (see above) except their portfolios contain the issues of only one state. A resident of that state has the advantage of receiving income free of both federal and state tax. For some taxpayers, portions of income from these securities may be subject to the federal alternative minimum tax.

U.S. Government Income Funds seek current income by investing in a variety of government securities. These include U.S. Treasury bonds, federally guaranteed mortgage-backed securities, and other government notes.

Source: *1994 Mutual Fund Fact Book*, Investment Company Institute, Washington, D.C. Reprinted with permission.

APPENDIX C

RESOURCES

Valuable sources of information available at your newsstand:

Newspapers:

Investors' Business Daily — In-depth statistical information on stocks and bonds. Particularly good coverage of mutual funds.

The New York Times — Superior coverage of the bond market and the Federal Reserve.

The Wall Street Journal — General financial news.

Magazines:

BARRON'S — Weekly coverage of foreign and domestic markets. Excellent statistics.

Forbes — Bi-weekly coverage of companies. Expert columnists give their market opinions.

Smart Money — Monthly, by the editors of *The Wall Street Journal*. Personal finance and investing written in laymen's terms.

Worth Magazine — Monthly, articles on personal finance and no-load mutual funds. Published by the owners of Fidelity Funds.

Newsletters - available only by subscription:

Dick Davis Digest — compendium of items of interest published in other financial newsletters—covers stocks and mutual funds. Write for a sample copy to:

Dick Davis Digest
P.O. Box 350630
Fort Lauderdale, FL 33335-0630

**NoLOAD FUND *X — excellent statistical coverage of no-load and low load mutual funds. Uses a statistical trend following technique for selecting funds for investment. Write for a sample copy to:

**NoLOAD FUND *X
235 Montgomery St.
San Francisco, CA 94104-2994

The No-Load Fund Investor — excellent statistical coverage of no-load and low load mutual funds. Also includes sample portfolios selected for investors with differing objectives. Subscription includes *The Handbook For No-Load Fund Investors.* The handbook is a gold mine of information. Write for a sample copy:

The No-Load Fund Investor, Inc.
PO Box 318
Irvington-on-Hudson, NY 10533

Morningstar — the single best source of statistical information on mutual funds for the serious investor. In-depth coverage on over 1,200 funds. Write for information to:

Morningstar
225 West Wacker Drive
Chicago, IL 60606

APPENDIX D

SAMPLE ACCOUNT HISTORY

History of a managed no-load mutual fund account with moderate growth objectives. Monthly performance rounded to nearest thousand dollars. Results include all transaction costs but are before deduction of management fees.

Month	End of month account value (000s)	Month	End of month account value (000s)
0	250	33	410
1	252	34	416
2	271	35	440
3	266	36	415
4	267	37	475
5	283	38	485
6	296	39	485
7	293	40	459
8	312	41	441
9	321	42	451
10	322	43	436
11	304	44	445
12	314	45	432
13	320	46	433
14	304	47	441
15	300	48	468
16	308	49	477
17	298	50	487
18	330	51	479
19	335	52	494
20	331	53	478
21	299	54	490
22	278	55	496
23	277	56	496
24	298	57	522
25	309	58	535
26	333	59	545
27	358	60	532
28	375	61	556
29	371	62	560
30	389	63	548
31	368	64	519
32	392	65	531

Cumulative gain since inception (65 months) +281,000   +111%

Compound Annual Growth Rate   + 15%

Months advancing   43
Months declining   22